VOICE

of

GOD

How To Hear It

CLEAR STEPS, REAL RESULTS

ISBN 979-8-9862426-1-3

Cover design: Jesus Is Too Real (JITR).
Published by Jesus Is Too Real (JITR).
Baltimore, Maryland

www.jesusistooreal.com

NO MORE GUESSING
HEAR GOD CLEARLY

VOICE of GOD

How To Hear It

CLEAR STEPS, REAL RESULTS

BY

OLA ABINA

DEDICATION

Dr. Elijah Abina & Matron Felicia Abina

My parents, whose lives exemplify the beauty of hearing and speaking God's voice as naturally as conversation itself. Your unwavering faith and wisdom continue to inspire.

ACKNOWLEDGMENTS

I want to thank my wife, Odalisa, for her sacrificial support,
which allows me the time to write this book.

Special thanks to my children—Abisola, Mishael, Israel, and Blessing—
for patiently bearing with me as I put many moments with them on hold
while working on this project.

To my Senior Pastor, Pastor Taiwo Fagbuyi, for deliberately providing
opportunities and modeling how to hear the voice of God with
precision—thank you.

To the Father, Son, and Holy Spirit—this is always about You. I write to
You, for You, and with You. You gave me the vision for this book.
Thank You for trusting me with this gift.

CONTENTS

CHAPTER 1

Read This Urgently

*"My sheep listen to my voice; I know them,
and they follow me."*

– JOHN 10:27 (NLT)

If You Can't Hear God's Voice, It Will Cost You.

Have you ever wished you could hear God's direction clearly? Have you ever wondered why some people confidently say, *"I heard God say…"* while you struggle to recognize His voice?

Maybe you've asked yourself:

"What am I missing? Why can't I hear Him like they do? Am I not a strong enough Christian?"

If this sounds familiar, you're not alone. I was once in the same place—desperate for answers, uncertain about how to recognize when God was speaking. But everything changed. I learned to hear His voice, and now, I want to show you how.

Source Yahoo! Finance.

Why Hearing God Matters

God's voice isn't just a spiritual luxury—it's a necessity. Not knowing what He's saying can lead to preventable losses and missed opportunities.

Take this example:

On **February 20, 2025,** I posted a TikTok video sharing a message I received from the Lord. He warned me that the **U.S. stock market would soon crash** and instructed me to stay out for the time being.

Then, on **April 3, 2025,** the market **began a downward spiral**. The **Wall Street Journal reported a staggering $6.6 trillion loss** in just two days.

Maybe you were affected by this. Maybe your investments took a hit, and you wondered afterward why you didn't see it coming. But what if you had heard God's voice warning just as He warned me?

A Pattern of Divine Warnings

This wasn't the first time God spoke to me about a major event. On **November 21, 2019,** months before the world knew anything about **COVID-19,** the Lord spoke again. He told me, **"Everyone should establish an online presence and embrace technology."** Businesses, churches, ministries, everyone needed to prepare.

I shared this revelation on my show, *Jesus Is Too Real,* and even published it in my book, *42 Financial Independence Laws for Christians.*

Then the pandemic hit.

Businesses that had shifted online **thrived**—while many who ignored the warning **collapsed overnight**.

Maybe you experienced this firsthand.

God Is Speaking—Are You Listening?

What if He's already speaking to you, but you haven't learned how to recognize His voice?

This happens to believers—seasoned Christians and new ones alike. Don't be discouraged. Hearing God's voice isn't reserved for a select few—it's for you, too.

The good news? You can learn to hear Him clearly, without guessing.

What You'll Discover in This Book

Hearing God's voice goes far beyond audible words. **His voice is any communication He sends to you.**

If you focus only on hearing an actual voice, you will miss the countless ways He speaks—through Scripture, dreams, visions, circumstances, inner impressions, and even His actions.

This book is designed to help you:

- Understand and identify divine communication with clarity.
- Stop second-guessing whether a thought or impression is truly from God.
- Discern between God's voice and your own mind.
- Recognize patterns in how He speaks.
- Learn methods to tune into His guidance daily.
- Activate ways for Him to speak to you in new ways.
- Validate messages to ensure they align with His truth.

It's Time to Stop Guessing

God **still speaks**, and He wants to guide you. He wants to give you specific instructions for your life, your family, your business, and your calling.

If you've ever wished you could hear Him more clearly—without doubting or wondering—this book is for you.

Let's begin.

CHAPTER 2

Hearing God's Voice Through Your Conscience

"And so, my dear friends, if our conscience does not condemn us, we have courage in God's presence."

— 1 JOHN 3:21 GNT

Have you ever wondered if God is speaking to you? Maybe you've prayed, waited, and hoped for some undeniable sign—a voice from heaven, a miraculous dream, or something so clear you couldn't miss it. But instead... silence. Or at least, it feels like silence. And that's frustrating, isn't it? When you're longing for clarity, for direction, all you hear is nothing.

What if the problem isn't that God is silent, but that you haven't learned to recognize how He speaks?

We often expect God's voice to sound a certain way. Loud, dramatic, unmistakable. But sometimes, God doesn't speak through noise. **He speaks through a nudge.**

And one of the most overlooked ways He communicates is through something He's already placed inside of you: **your conscience**.

What Is the Conscience?

Your conscience is that inner sense of right and wrong. God's whisper within you.

It's more than just thoughts or emotions. It's God's built-in warning system: a quiet, persistent guide that steers you toward wisdom and away from regret.

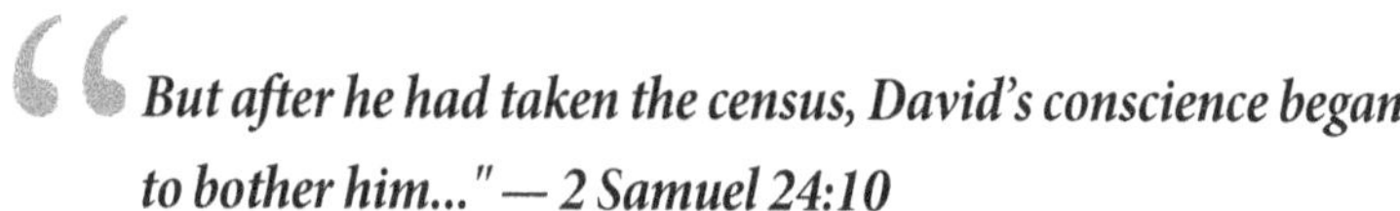

> *But after he had taken the census, David's conscience began to bother him..." — 2 Samuel 24:10*

Sometimes it flashes a red light before you act, urging you to pause. Other times, it weighs heavy after the fact, calling you to repentance.

When your conscience stirs, God is often behind it.

Why Does God Speak Through the Conscience?

God knows life moves fast. You can't always wait for a vision or a prophetic word. So, He's given you a built-in compass to help steer you in real time.

God uses your conscience:

- To guard your decisions
- To restrain your reactions
- To convict your heart
- To draw you back when you wander

Unlike external signs or audible voices, your conscience is always with you. It's God's consistent, quiet voice on the inside.

How God Speaks Through Your Conscience

1. Unease Before an Action

Have you ever hesitated before saying something, sharing a thought, or making a decision? That hesitation, the tension you feel deep in your spirit, is often God's way of stopping you before a mistake. That uneasy feeling? It's not random. It's God, gently restraining you.

2. Conviction Afterward

Another way God speaks through your conscience is after the fact.

Maybe you snapped at someone. Ignored a nudge to help. Said something reckless. At first, it seems minor. But as time passes, you feel that uncomfortable tension, that deep regret. I've been there too.

There was a time I let pride stop me from apologizing. I told myself, *"It's not a big deal. They'll get over it."* Days passed, but the heaviness didn't. Finally, I reached out and apologized. Instantly, the weight lifted.

That conviction? That was God, leading me toward repentance.

BIBLICAL EXAMPLE: David's Troubled Conscience

Even David, a man after God's own heart experienced the sting of conscience.

King Saul had been hunting him down, trying to kill him. Then one day, Saul unknowingly stepped into the very cave where David and his men were hiding. David could have ended it all with one strike. Instead, he cut off a piece of Saul's robe.

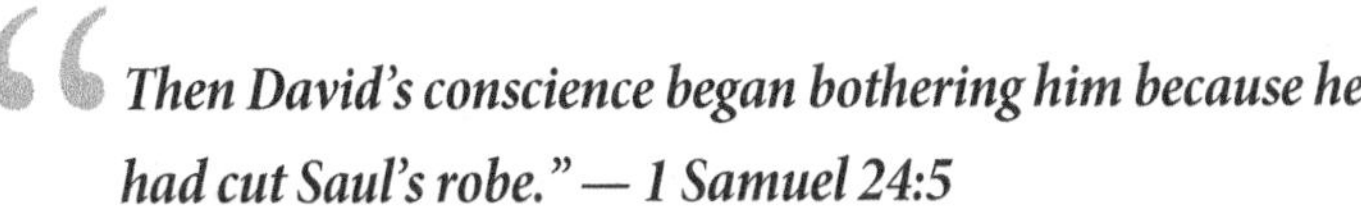

> *Then David's conscience began bothering him because he had cut Saul's robe." — 1 Samuel 24:5*

What he did seemed small. But David knew he had crossed a line. It wasn't about the robe—it was about **honor**. Saul was still God's anointed. **Sometimes, what seems small to us matters deeply to God.**

REAL LIFE RESULT – Hearing God Before I Hit 'Post'

I've experienced firsthand how God speaks through my conscience.

Being active online and sharing Christian content, I receive both encouragement and harsh criticism. Some critiques are fair. Others? Mocking, misrepresenting, even outright false accusations. And I'm human. So, sometimes, I want to clap back.

One day, an incident occurred, and I felt the urge to respond. I picked up my phone, started typing, ready to defend myself. But then... I paused. Something shifted inside me—a weight, a tension. It was God nudging me: *"Is this how I want you to respond? Is this what reflects Me?"*

In that moment, I deleted every word. Because I couldn't post it in good conscience.

How to Position Yourself to Hear God Through Your Conscience

- **Obey Quickly** – The more you obey, the clearer it becomes. The more you delay, the harder it is to hear.
- **Stay in God's Word** – Scripture tunes your conscience to truth.
- **Pray for Sensitivity** – Ask God to soften your heart daily.
- **Repent Fast** – Don't linger in conviction. Restoration starts with surrender.

Best Practices for Discernment

- Slow down before important decisions.
- Pay attention to inner tension not just logic.

- Journal moments of conviction and how you responded.
- Invite accountability. Godly counsel sharpens sensitivity.
- Stay humble. A teachable heart keeps your conscience alive.

Reflective Bridge

Maybe you've been brushing off that small check in your spirit or talking yourself out of that sense of unease. But now, you recognize it wasn't just your thoughts. It was God.

Encouragement

Your conscience is more than just a feeling. It's a **divine instrument for direction**. Don't dismiss those quiet checks in your spirit. Don't ignore the unease. And when conviction comes, don't fear it. **It's proof that God hasn't gone silent.**

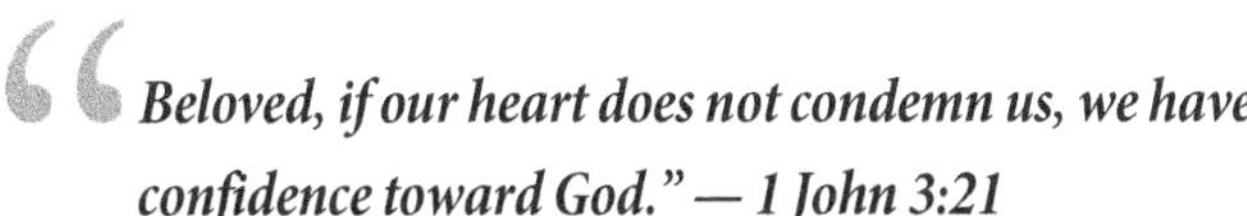

> *Beloved, if our heart does not condemn us, we have confidence toward God." — 1 John 3:21*

Reflection Questions

- Have you ignored your conscience recently?
- Is there an apology or correction you've been avoiding?
- What is one area where you can begin obeying that inner voice today?

Closing Prayer

"Lord, help me hear Your voice through my conscience. Keep my heart soft and willing to listen. Give me the courage to obey when You nudge me. Lead me deeper into Your truth. In Jesus' name, Amen."

CHAPTER 3

Hearing God's Voice Through Peace

"You will go out in joy and be led forth in peace…"

— ISAIAH 55:12

Have you ever had to make a decision that looked perfect on the outside but left you unsettled inside? Maybe the numbers added up. Maybe the people around you said it was the right move. But something in your spirit whispered, *"Not yet."*

Or maybe, in the middle of chaos, you felt strangely calm, peaceful even. That peace didn't come from your circumstances. It came from somewhere deeper.

That stillness? That hesitation? That calm confidence? That is God speaking through peace.

We often look for God's voice in the spectacular—fire from heaven, prophetic dreams, loud declarations. But sometimes, His guidance comes in quiet clarity. He leads with peace.

Peace isn't a passive emotion—it's an active direction from God.

What Is Peace?

Peace is not simply the absence of conflict or anxiety. It's the presence of divine alignment.

In Hebrew, the word *shalom* means wholeness, completeness, and harmony. It's a deep inner knowing that God is in control—and you're walking in step with Him.

> " *The peace of God, which surpasses all understanding, will guard your hearts and minds in Christ Jesus." —* *Philippians 4:7*

Peace is more than a feeling. It's a confirmation from the Holy Spirit.

Why Does God Speak Through Peace?

God is not the author of confusion (1 Corinthians 14:33). He wants us to walk in confidence, not chaos.

Here's why peace is one of God's favorite ways to guide His people:

- Peace slows you down when you want to rush.
- Peace protects you from manipulation or pressure.
- Peace confirms when something is in line with God's will.
- Peace becomes your internal compass when external signs are unclear.

When everything around you are loud and fast, God often speaks through stillness.

How God Speaks Through Peace

1. Peace That Doesn't Make Sense

There are times when you're in a situation that *should* make you panic, but you're calm. You feel anchored. You feel protected. That's not numbness. It's God leading you through His supernatural peace. He may not speak with words, but He will flood your spirit with calm. That's how you know He's present.

2. Unease You Can't Explain

Sometimes, God leads by withdrawing His peace from you in a situation. Everything looks good on paper. Everyone is excited. The door is open. But you feel unsettled inside. That is God leading you.

BIBLICAL EXAMPLE: Jesus In a Storm

> *Let the peace of Christ rule in your hearts..."* — *Colossians 3:15*

Peace isn't passive. It's active. It helps you know when to step forward and when to stand still.

Jesus modeled this perfectly. During a life-threatening storm, while His disciples panicked, Jesus slept. Why? Because He was filled with peace. His peace didn't come from calm waters. It came from His connection to the Father.

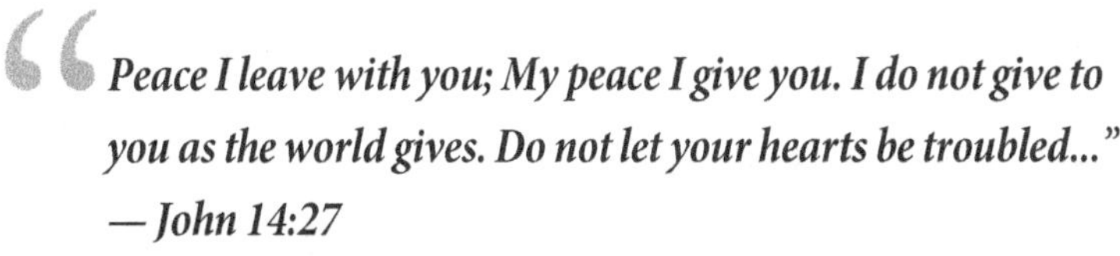

> *Peace I leave with you; My peace I give you. I do not give to you as the world gives. Do not let your hearts be troubled..."* — *John 14:27*

REAL LIFE RESULT – No Peace, No Go

A few years ago, I was offered a ministry speaking opportunity that looked ideal—an influential platform, a generous honorarium, and a wide audience.

Even my wife asked, *"Have you prayed about this?"* I had. But there was no dramatic word. No confirming dream. Just silence. And in that silence, there was no peace.

My spirit felt tight and restless. I couldn't shake the unease. I just didn't have peace.

Then one evening, it clicked. God had already spoken. Weeks earlier, He had given me specific instructions about what to focus on in that season. This opportunity, though good, would've pulled me off course. So, I declined. And immediately, that inner pressure lifted.

Sometimes the absence of peace is God reminding you of what He's already said.

That moment taught me: no peace means no go.

How to Position Yourself to Hear God Through Peace

- **Create Quietness** - Noise drowns stillness. Turn down the volume around you.
- **Surrender Your Bias** - Ask God to override your preferences with His will.
- **Don't Rush** – Peace grows in patience. Pressure drowns clarity.
- **Seek God First** – Peace flows from relationship, not formulas.

Best Practices for Discernment

- Write down your options. Which direction brings stillness?
- Don't decide when you feel emotionally charged.

- Compare each decision with Scripture.
- Check for conflict with past instructions. Peace won't override what God already told you.
- Wait if peace is missing. Sometimes, stillness is the answer.

Reflective Bridge

Has God been trying to lead you through peace, but you've been pushing past it? Maybe you've been ignoring peace because it doesn't feel urgent. But what if peace is God's most urgent way of leading you, quiet, but firm?

Encouragement

God's peace is more than a calm feeling. It's a spiritual signal. It may not come with a voice or a vision, but when His peace shows up, follow it. If peace leads, you can walk with confidence even when the path isn't fully clear.

 *You will go out in joy and be led forth in peace." — Isaiah 55:12*

Reflection Questions

- When was the last time you overrode peace and regretted it?
- Are you currently facing a decision where peace is missing?
- What step can you take to slow down and invite peace back in?

Closing Prayer

"Lord, speak to me through Your peace. Still my heart when I'm anxious. Restrain me when I'm rushing. Lead me with quiet confidence. Teach me to follow Your peace more than my preferences. In Jesus' name, Amen."

Hearing God Through the Bible

"For the word of God is alive and powerful. It is sharper than the sharpest two-edged sword… It exposes our innermost thoughts and desires."

— HEBREWS 4:12 (NLT)

You've been desperate. You've cried. You've prayed through tears and confusion, longing for God to speak. Wouldn't it be easier if He just texted you clear directions?

The truth is… He already has. The Bible is God's voice in written form, alive, relevant, and dependable. You were never meant to guess. If there's one method you can trust completely, it's this: **God's Word is the most trustworthy, infallible way He speaks.**

What Is the Bible as a Method of Hearing God?

The Bible is more than a book. It's a living document where God speaks daily. Unlike impressions or dreams that may need discernment, Scripture is already verified truth. It anchors every other method of hearing God.

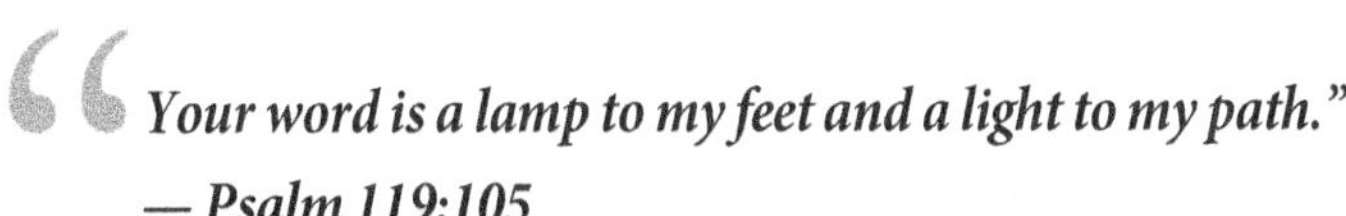

Your word is a lamp to my feet and a light to my path."
— Psalm 119:105

Why Does God Speak Through the Bible?

Because the Bible never changes. It is reliable, foundational, and aligned with His nature. Every other method must submit to it.

> *For God is not the author of confusion but of peace…"*
> *— 1 Corinthians 14:33 (KJV)*

> *You have magnified Your word above all Your name."*
> *— Psalm 138:2 (NKJV)*

If you want clarity, start here.

How God Might Speak to You Through the Bible

1. Instant Illumination

> *The entrance of Your words gives light." — Psalm 119:130*

Sometimes you read a verse and suddenly everything clicks. A light goes on. You see the path ahead clearly. Pause, reflect, and receive what He's revealing.

2. Spotlight Moments

Sometimes, a verse keeps showing up to you, in sermons, posts, conversations. It keeps following you. When the same scripture shows up multiple times, God is emphasizing something. Pay attention to it.

3. Unsettling or Confusing Scriptures

Another way that God often speaks is through scriptures that would challenge you. Have you ever read something in the Bible that bothered you? Or didn't make sense? Don't skip over it. Think of Moses and the burning bush. God didn't speak *until* Moses turned aside to investigate. (Exodus 3:4). Sometimes revelation follows curiosity.

That "hard" verse may contain a treasure.

- Read the full chapter for context.
- Cross-reference with other scriptures.
- Ask a trusted, mature believer.
- Some of the richest revelations come from wrestling, not rushing.

4. Repetition in Your Spirit

Another way God speaks is repeating scriptures in your spirit. Did you find yourself keep thinking about the same verse even without trying to. That's the Holy Spirit bringing God's Word back to your attention.

- Meditate on it
- Write it down
- Ask God, *"What are You showing me?"*

5. Scripture That Grows With You

The Bible isn't static. It grows with you. A verse that meant one thing years ago may suddenly hit deeper today. Why? Because as you mature spiritually, God reveals more layers of His truth. The Bible is living. It adapts to your season and speaks into your growth.

BIBLICAL EXAMPLE – Joshua: Guided by God's Word for Victory

Joshua is a powerful example of a biblical character who relied on Scripture for direction.

When He took over leadership after Moses, he faced the huge task of leading Israel into the Promised Land. God gave him a clear instruction:

> *This Book of the Law shall not depart from your mouth, but you shall meditate on it day and night, so that you may be careful to do everything written in it. Then you will be prosperous and successful." — (Joshua 1:8) NKJV.*

Joshua didn't rely on his own wisdom. He consulted God's Word as his guide. He meditated on it, obeyed it, and used it to make decisions.

One example of Joshua applying Scriptural direction was during the battle of Jericho (Joshua 6). Instead of using conventional warfare tactics, he followed God's instructions, which aligned with divine principles. The Israelites marched around the city for seven days, just as God commanded, and the walls supernaturally collapsed.

Joshua's success wasn't based on military strategy alone. It was rooted in his obedience to God's written Word. His story teaches us that Scripture is a reliable source of direction, and when we follow it, we walk in God's promises.

REAL LIFE RESULT – How God's Word Multiplied My Provision

Not long ago, I found myself in a financial bind. I had prayed, asking God for a very specific amount. I listed my needs, explained the urgency, and fully expected a direct, miraculous provision.

But when the answer came, it was underwhelming. The money I received wasn't enough. It was just a fraction of what I'd asked for. I was grateful but confused. Had God heard me? Was this a test?

One day while reading Scripture, I came across the familiar story of Jesus feeding the five thousand. It stood out. Not just the miracle, but the beginning: five loaves and two fish. A boy's lunch. Barely anything compared to the massive need.

Yet Jesus didn't reject it. He didn't complain. Instead, He had the people sit, and He gave thanks for what little they had. Then, as He broke the bread and distributed it, it multiplied.

That was my moment of illumination. I felt like the Holy Spirit turned a light on in my spirit: *"God is not ignoring your need. He's waiting for your gratitude to unlock the multiplication."*

So I changed course. I began to thank God deeply and sincerely for the small provision. I worshipped and declared that He was my provider.

Not long after, the rest of the money came in unexpected ways and from unexpected sources. It wasn't just enough. It was more than enough.

God's Word had spoken clearly. And when I aligned with it, my situation turned around.

How to Position Yourself to Hear God Through the Bible

1. **Start with Prayer** – Ask, "Speak, Lord. I'm listening."
2. **Use a Reading Plan** – Consistency opens clarity.
3. **Read Slowly** – Don't rush. God speaks in pauses.
4. **Journal What Stands Out** – Capture what you sense.
5. **Study in Context** – Don't cherry-pick. Understand the whole.
6. **Ask the Holy Spirit for Interpretation** – He knows what the Father is saying.
7. **Use the S.O.A.P. Method** – Scripture, Observation, Application, Prayer.

Best Practices for Discernment

Here's how to keep your hearing sharp and avoid confusion as you engage with Scripture:

- Never twist Scripture to fit your preference. Let it confront you and correct you.
- Check for repetition. If a verse keeps coming up, God is emphasizing it.
- Stay submitted to the whole Bible, not just your favorite parts. Balance is safety.
- Let Scripture interpret Scripture. Use cross-references to get the full picture.
- Be cautious of "random verse roulette." Context matters more than convenience.
- Confirm impressions with Scripture. If your "leading" contradicts the Bible, it's not from God.
- Talk it out with trusted believers. God often confirms His Word in community.

Reflective Bridge

Have you skipped over certain Scripture verses, rushed through devotionals, or overlooked messages that you now feel drawn to revisit? That's God already trying to get your attention. Take a moment to recognize it and respond in obedience.

Encouragement

Don't just ask for a word. Open the Word. God's voice is not a mystery when you know where to listen.

"The Bible is the safest, clearest, and most consistent way God speaks."
"Clarity is possible."

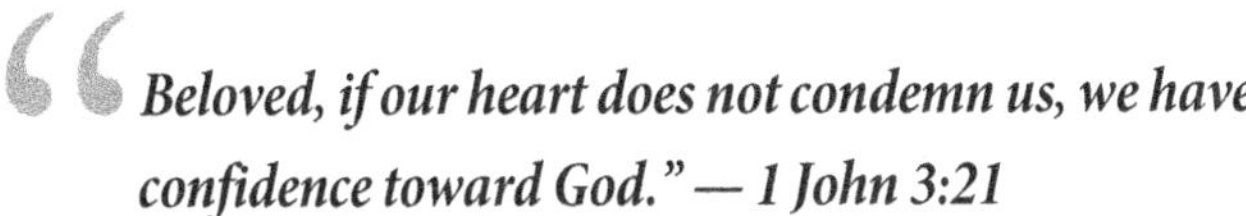

Beloved, if our heart does not condemn us, we have confidence toward God." — 1 John 3:21

Reflection Questions

- When was the last time a verse spoke directly to your situation?
- Is there a verse or passage God keeps bringing back to you?
- What's one way you can create more space for Scripture this week?

Closing Prayer

"Lord, open my heart to Your Word. Let it come alive. Teach me to listen, to slow down, and to believe that You are speaking through every page. Help me hear clearly, obey quickly, and love Your truth. In Jesus' name, Amen."

CHAPTER 5

Hearing the Voice of God Through Prayer

"The Lord is near to all who call on him, to all who call on him in truth."

— Psalm 145:18

Is Your Prayer a One-Way Conversation?

You've cried. You've pleaded. You've prayed with tears running down your face... and still—nothing. Isn't it frustrating to feel like heaven is silent? Maybe you've asked, *"Lord, are You even listening?"*

If you've ever felt that way, you're not alone. Many believers have wrestled with the silence that sometimes follows prayer. But here's what most don't realize:

Prayer is not a one-sided monologue. God doesn't just listen—He answers.

Clarity in prayer is possible. You just need to know where to listen.

God isn't distant or disinterested. He's present and willing to speak. The real question is: Are you making space to listen?

What Is Prayer?

Prayer is more than just asking. It's aligning. It's not just unloading your worries. It's engaging in deep, spiritual connection with the Creator of the universe.

Think about your closest relationships. You don't just talk, you listen. You feel. You respond. The more time you spend together, the more connected you become.

God desires that same closeness. Not just to hear from you, but **to share His heart with you.**

Why Does God Speak Through Prayer?

Prayer is one of the most intimate moments between you and God. It's where:

- He confirms that He hears you (Psalm 34:17)
- He provides direction (Proverbs 3:5-6)
- He strengthens your faith (Philippians 4:6-7)
- He reveals His desires (James 1:5)

You speak. He listens. He speaks. You learn to recognize.

God responds in the stillness, in the sacred pauses, in the humble spaces of surrendered prayer.

How God Might Speak to You Through Prayer

Through Prophecy

Have you ever had someone pray over you and say something that pierced right to the core of your situation? Something they couldn't have known. That could be God using them as a vessel.

Acts 13:1–3 describes a powerful moment of corporate prayer and fasting. During that time, the Holy Spirit clearly spoke to the group:

> *Appoint Barnabas and Saul for the special work to which I have called them." — Acts 13:2*

God still speaks like this today.

Thought Implantation

You're praying and suddenly a clear, profound thought enters your mind. It is almost like a divine whisper. These thoughts often carry a weight of clarity, conviction, or direction that ordinary ideas lack. They don't just pass through. They settle in your spirit. It wasn't random. It was God planting insight into your spirit.

Audible Voice

There are also moments in prayer when God speaks in an audible voice that is unmistakably clear to the physical ear.

In Exodus 14:15, we see God responding directly to Moses in a moment of desperation:

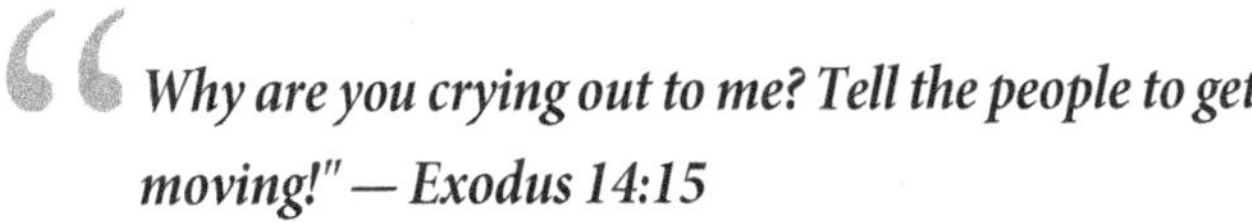

> *Why are you crying out to me? Tell the people to get moving!" — Exodus 14:15*

It is possible to hear God's voice so clearly that you turn around thinking someone was in the room. His voice still breaks through when necessary.

Trance or Vision

While in deep prayer, God sometimes may speak to you visually. It could be like a scene, image, or symbol but with spiritual meaning.

Acts 22:17 tells of Paul falling into a trance while praying in the temple. In that moment, God gave him a clear and personal vision:

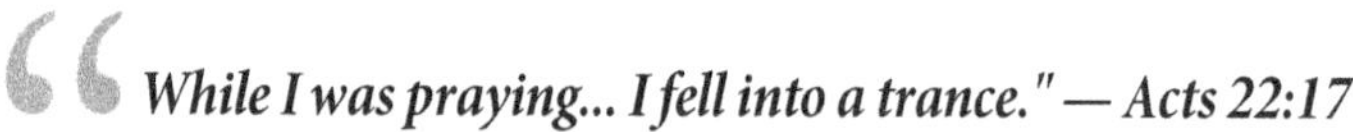

While I was praying... I fell into a trance." — Acts 22:17

These divine visuals can bring you clarity, correction, or calling. They could guide you toward God's next steps.

Through Peace

...Then you will experience God's peace, which exceeds anything we can understand." — Philippians 4:7

Have you ever ended a prayer with a supernatural peace, calmness that you didn't have when you started? That peace, that deep assurance is His voice. It may not come through words, but it speaks with power.

Through Dreams

God could also speak to you in dreams after praying. 1 Kings 3:5 tells us that God spoke to Solomon in a dream after he prayed and made sacrifices.

Maybe you've experienced this. A dream so vivid that it stayed with you, lining up with what you'd been praying about. That could have been God responding to your prayer.

Through Signs and Wonders

When Elijah prayed for rain (1 Kings 18:42–44), he didn't get thunder or a storm right away. Instead, his servant saw something small. Just a cloud the size of a man's hand. But that little sign carried a big meaning.

God often answers gradually through subtle changes in circumstances, unexpected encouragement, or even delays that teach dependence. Don't miss the small signs. They often mark the beginning of a divine response. Your answer may not be immediate. Instead, it may start as subtle shifts in your situation.

Through Other People

Sometimes God speaks through others to you after you have prayed. It is often when you least expect it.

When Hannah was crying out in desperation for a child (1 Samuel 1:12–17), it was Eli the priest who confirmed that God had heard her. He didn't know what she had prayed, but God used him to affirm His response.

In the same way, a mentor, friend, pastor, or even a stranger might unknowingly speak directly into your situation. If their words echo what you've been praying about, don't brush it off. God may be answering you through them.

BIBLICAL EXAMPLE – Solomon: A Prayer, A Dream, A Destiny

When Solomon became king, he had a huge responsibility, leading an entire nation. He knew he couldn't do it alone, so he prayed offered sacrifice seeking God's guidance.

That night, as he slept in **Gibeon**, God appeared to him **in a dream**.

> *At Gibeon, the Lord appeared to Solomon in a dream by night, and God said, 'Ask what I shall give you.'"*
> *(1 Kings 3:5)*

God gave Solomon an incredible opportunity: **Ask for anything, and it will be yours.**

He asked for **wisdom**. The ability to govern God's people well. God was pleased with his request.

> *Since you have asked for wisdom… I will give you a wise and discerning heart, so that there has never been anyone like you, nor will there ever be."* *(1 Kings 3:11-12)*

That dream wasn't random. It was God directly answering Solomon's prayer. Because of it, Solomon became known as the wisest king in Israel's history.

His story teaches us that God can answer prayers in dreams. If you've been asking God for direction, clarity, or wisdom, don't ignore the quiet ways He may already be answering. God may already be speaking to you in ways you didn't expect. You just need to recognize it.

REAL LIFE RESULT – When God Spoke Through Signs & Wonders

I'll never forget a moment when prayer became more than words. when it opened the door for a miracle...

Sometime ago, my phone rang. On the other end was panic. The voice was frantic, desperate. A loved one struggling to explain through tears and confusion. It was about a little girl I deeply care about. Her body had gone limp, her eyes rolled back, and her skin turned pale. They were watching life slip from her.

I tried to stay calm as I listened, but my spirit was stirred. I didn't panic. Instead, I turned to what I know works: worship.

I began to magnify God. I praised Him for His faithfulness, for the miracles He had already done in her life. I declared His greatness, not the crisis. That's one of my spiritual strategies. Start every urgent prayer with worship. It invites God into the situation. It shifts my focus off fear and onto His power. **Worship shifts your focus from panic to presence.** It confuses the enemy.

As worship continued, something happened within me. Faith rose. I didn't even ask yet. I just told them to check on her again.

And then it happened. She stirred. Her body responded. She came back.

Before a word of petition left my lips, God moved. He answered through signs wonders.

How to Position Yourself to Hear God Through Prayer

- **Pray Expectantly** – Come ready to hear, not just speak.
- **Engage in Worship** – Start by lifting Him, not your problems.
- **Practice Silence** – Don't rush to end the moment—listen.
- **Journal Impressions** – Capture thoughts, scriptures, nudges.
- **Seek Confirmation** – God's voice always aligns with His character and Word.
- **Avoid Panic-Prayers** – Anchor your heart before making your request.

Best Practices for Discernment

- Pause often while praying - Let silence speak.
- End with stillness - Create room for response.
- Use instrumental worship- It helps maintain focus.

- Write everything down- Clarity often comes after reflection.
- Test every impression- Does it line up with God's Word?

Reflective Bridge

Have you been looking in the wrong places for answer to your prayers? Now you can stop guessing and start recognizing that clarity in prayer is possible.

Encouragement

Don't just walk away from prayer hoping God heard you. Walk away expecting that He will speak. Maybe not in the way you imagined, but always in the way you need. Prayer isn't a ritual. It's a relationship. And relationships thrive on communication.

You were never meant to guess your way through prayer. God is speaking—now you know how to hear Him.

Reflection Questions

- Have you ever sensed God's voice in prayer?
- Which of these ways has He spoken to you before?
- What steps can you take to hear Him more clearly?

Closing Prayer

"Lord, teach me to listen when I pray. Open my heart to recognize Your voice—whether through Scripture, peace, prophecy, or even silence. Give me wisdom to discern, patience to wait, and courage to obey. In Jesus' name, Amen."

CHAPTER 6

Hearing the Voice of God Through Dreams

"In a dream, in a vision of the night… He may speak in their ears and terrify them with warnings."

— JOB 33:15

Have you ever woken up from a dream you couldn't shake? The details were vivid. The emotions stayed. It felt like more than just your imagination. What if it was God speaking?

Dreams may seem random, but not all are. Some are spiritual messages waiting to be decoded. In this chapter, we'll explore how to recognize God's voice through dreams so you can stop guessing and start discerning.

What Are God-Given Dreams?

Dreams are one of the oldest, most consistent ways God speaks. They bypass your conscious mind and speak directly to your spirit.

> *For God speaks again and again, though people do not recognize it. He speaks in dreams, in visions of the night…"*
> *— Job 33:14–15 (NLT)*

God-given dreams:

- **Reveal His will** – Divine direction for decisions or the future.
- **Warn of danger** – Alerting you to deception or spiritual attack.
- **Confirm His word** – Reinforcing what you've heard in prayer.
- **Bring encouragement** – Comfort in times of fear or confusion.

Why Does God Speak Through Dreams?

God speaks in a dream because when we sleep, we quiet the distractions of daily life. Our body rests and our spirit is often most receptive.

Also, God speaks through dreams to:

Warn and Instruct

God can use your dream to give you instructions or warn you in a matter of life or death for you or your loved ones.

In the Bible, God spoke in a dream through an angel to Joseph, the earthly father of baby Jesus. He instructed him to take the child and flee to Egypt to escape Herod's attempt to kill Him.

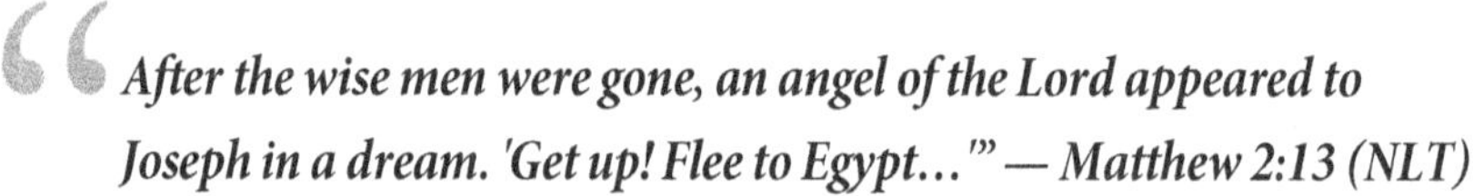

After the wise men were gone, an angel of the Lord appeared to Joseph in a dream. 'Get up! Flee to Egypt...'" — Matthew 2:13 (NLT)

Today, God still warns through dreams. He may urge you to delay a journey, stay home, or take a different route to avoid danger. It may not come with thunder, but the peace and urgency in the dream can be unmistakably divine.

Reveal The Future

God can also use your dreams to reveal your future to you. These are called prophetic dreams because they foretell what is to come.

In the Bible, Joseph, the son of Jacob (Israel), had several dreams that predicted his future. Once he interpreted them, he knew he was destined to be a ruler.

> 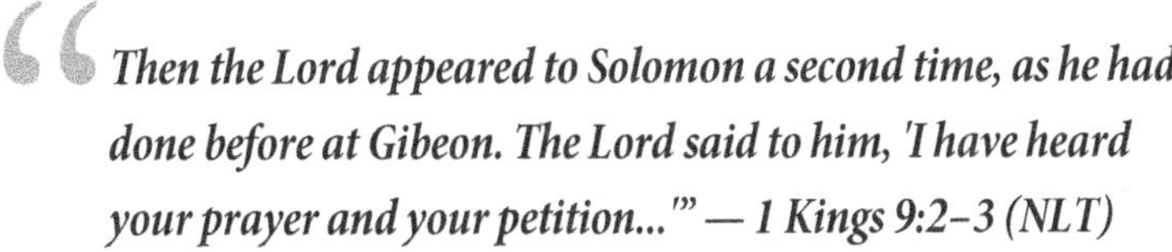
> *Soon Joseph had another dream, and again he told his brothers about it. 'Listen, I have had another dream,' he said. 'The sun, moon, and eleven stars bowed low before me!' This time he told the dream to his father as well as to his brothers, but his father scolded him. 'What kind of dream is that?' he asked. 'Will your mother and I and your brothers actually come and bow to the ground before you?'"*
> *— Genesis 37:9–10 (NLT)*

God still gives such dreams today to reveal purpose, calling, and destiny. They may not always be fully understood at first, but when recorded and discerned, they unfold powerfully over time.

Answer Prayers

If you have prayed to God about something, He might answer you through a dream.

King Solomon prayed to God, and God answered him in a dream:

> *Then the Lord appeared to Solomon a second time, as he had done before at Gibeon. The Lord said to him, 'I have heard your prayer and your petition...'"* *— 1 Kings 9:2–3 (NLT)*

God still answers prayers through dreams today. He doesn't need to physically appear in your dreams for you to know He's answered. He may use symbols instead.

For example, if you've prayed about your finances and then dreamt of receiving or wearing new clothes, that could be God's way of saying your status is about to change. Remember Joseph? Before he appeared before Pharaoh, his prison clothes were changed—and he never wore them again.

Lead To Financial Fortune

God can also use your dreams to lead you into wealth and provision. King Solomon became the richest man who ever lived because of a dream.

> *That night the Lord appeared to Solomon in a dream, and God said, 'What do you want? Ask, and I will give it to you!' …So God replied… 'I will give you what you asked for! I will give you a wise and understanding heart such as no one else has had or ever will have! And I will also give you what you did not ask for—riches and fame!'"*
> *— 1 Kings 3:5, 11–13 (NLT)*

God still gives such dreams today. Larry Page, co-founder of Google, had a dream at age 23 about downloading the entire internet with links. He woke up, grabbed a pen, and wrote the idea down. That idea eventually became Google—now worth over $2 trillion. Larry Page's personal fortune is over $136 billion.

God can speak practically, not just spiritually.

How God Speaks Through Dreams

God speaks through dreams in two major ways: directly or indirectly. Directly means the dream requires virtually no interpretation. These are very rare. Indirectly means the dream requires interpretation. This is the norm. It could include symbols, numbers, colors, objects, animals, people, things, events etc.

Many dreams are simply the result of daily activity, stress, or subconscious processing. That's why discernment and interpretation are key. To understand what God is saying to you in a dream, it must be interpreted in the context of what is going on in your life.

Steps for Dream Interpretation:

1. First, note your initial reaction or impression when you woke up from your dream. Were you joyful, excited, or afraid and confused?
2. Begin the process of isolation and elimination. Divide your dream into sections.
3. Does your dream have a main concept or action that occurred?
4. If it does, who performed the action or didn't act?
5. What were you or the person doing or not doing?
6. What was the outcome of the dream, victory, defeat, uncertainty, success, or failure?
7. Are there numbers written or mentioned?
8. Were there colors written, mentioned, worn, or seen?
9. Were there animals or objects?
10. Pray for interpretation.
11. Identify what is currently going on in your life that could provide context for the dream.

For more about how to interpret dreams including symbols, signs, colors, and numbers, I've written a bestselling book on biblical dream interpretation. You can get a copy here: https://a.co/d/3iDNhrv

BIBLICAL EXAMPLE: How God Helped Jacob Grow His Business

Jacob worked hard for years, taking care of his father-in-law Laban's flocks. But no matter how much effort he put in, he wasn't getting ahead. Laban kept changing his wages, making it almost impossible for Jacob to build wealth.

Then one night, God stepped in.

Jacob had a dream. In it, he saw streaked, speckled, and spotted animals mating—something unusual.

> *One time during the mating season, I had a dream and saw that the male goats mating with the females were streaked, speckled, and spotted." (Genesis 31:10)*

Through this dream, God showed Jacob a strategy. A way to build his business and increase his wealth. Jacob followed what he saw, placing striped branches in front of his flocks during mating season. Soon, the strongest animals started producing speckled and spotted offspring. And those animals? They belonged to Jacob.

> *As a result, Jacob became very wealthy, with large flocks of sheep and goats, female and male servants, and many camels and donkeys." (Genesis 30:43)*

What seemed like a small dream was actually a divine business plan. God gave Jacob supernatural wisdom, helping him outsmart Laban and build lasting success.

God can give you business ideas too. If you've been asking for guidance on your finances or work, pay attention. He may already be speaking to you in ways you didn't expect.

REAL LIFE RESULT – How God Revealed Our Daughter's Birth

Dreams are one of the main ways God speaks to me. Because I've seen so many come to pass, I keep a dream and revelations journal.

Some years ago, I had a vivid dream that we were going to have a baby girl. In that same dream, I also saw her name. At the time, my wife wasn't pregnant, and we weren't planning for more children. We already had some. But the dream felt significant. It was too detailed, too specific to ignore. I knew it was God speaking.

So, I wrote it down.

Months later, to our surprise, my wife became pregnant. When we went for an ultrasound, we were told it was a girl. Just as the dream had revealed. And when she was born, we named her exactly what I had seen in the dream: Blessing.

That name came from heaven before she ever arrived on earth.

Dreams are not always random. They can be God's way of speaking directly to you. Have you ever had a dream like that? One that felt bigger than just imagination?

How to Position Yourself to Hear God Through Dreams

- **Be Mindful Before You Sleep** - Be mindful of what you watch or hear prior to going to sleep. They could pollute your dream.
- **Pray Before You Sleep** – Ask God to speak clearly to you while you sleep.

- **Recall Your Dream** - Recall your dream prior to opening your eyes. Some dreams are sensitive to light, sounds or sudden movements.
- **Write Down Your Dreams** – Write dreams down as soon as you wake up.
- **Pray For Interpretation** - Pray to God for His interpretation.
- **Reflect** – Reflect in the context of your life. Don't rush to conclusions.

Best Practices for Discernment

Dreams can stir emotions, offer insights, or even feel divine, but not all come from God. That's why discerning their source is essential. God will never contradict Himself or lead you in confusion.

- Pray for Interpretation – Ask God what the dream means.
- Compare with Scripture – God won't contradict His Word.
- Seek Confirmation – Through wise counsel or repetition.
- Write It Down – Patterns often emerge over time.
- Don't Act on Impulse – Wisdom often waits.

Reflective Bridge

Maybe you've had dreams that left you wondering, *"Was that from God?"* Maybe you've brushed off messages meant to guide you. But now, you can begin recognizing the voice of God even in your sleep.

Encouragement

God may be speaking when you least expect it even while you sleep. Don't ignore your dreams. Pray, seek wisdom, and allow God to reveal His truth. God may not always repeat Himself. When He speaks listen.

Reflection Questions

- Have you ever had a dream that felt like God was speaking?
- How can you grow in discernment to recognize God-given dreams?
- What steps can you take to respond when a dream carries spiritual significance?

Closing Prayer

"Lord, if You choose to speak to me through dreams, help me to recognize Your voice. Give me wisdom to discern what is from You. Reveal Your truth to me, and guide me in how to respond. In Jesus' name, Amen."

CHAPTER 7

Hearing God Through Closed Visions

"The Lord said, 'Go over to Straight Street, to the house of Judas. When you get there, ask for a man from Tarsus named Saul. He is praying to me right now. I have shown him a vision of a man named Ananias coming in and laying hands on him so he can see again.'"

— ACTS 9:11–12

Prayer and worship can be deeply personal moments. Times when your heart is open and your mind is focused on God. But sometimes, in those quiet spaces, something unexpected happens.

Your eyes are closed, yet you **see** something. Not with your physical eyes, but in your spirit. A flash of light, a picture, a scene, or even a person. It's vivid and clear, yet you weren't thinking about it moments before.

These moments aren't just random. God is trying to show you something just like He did with Saul on Straight Street. This is what's known as a **closed vision**. Your eyes are shut, but your spirit sees.

What Is a Closed Vision?

A closed vision is a supernatural image, scene, or revelation given by God while your eyes are physically shut but your mind is completely alert. These often happen during prayer, worship, or quiet reflection. They are distinct from dreams (which happen in sleep) or night visions (which occur in a semi-sleep state).

These moments are not imagined or conjured. They break into your awareness, carrying heaven's clarity, conviction, or comfort.

Why Does God Speak Through Closed Visions?

To Answer Prayer

God may send a vision while you're praying, revealing insight, direction, or assurance just as He did for Saul in Acts 9.

To Give Direction

He may show you a literal or symbolic path when you're unsure which way to go.

To Encourage or Warn

Closed visions can lift your heart or protect your path.

> *I have shown him a vision…" – Acts 9:12*

How God Might Speak to You Through Closed Visions

While some closed visions maybe direct and straightforward, the majority would be symbolic requiring interpretation.

1. Direct Vision

At times, a closed vision may come to you with an accompanying voice or impression, explaining its meaning immediately. This type of vision often requires quick action or obedience.

2. Symbolic Vision

Some closed visions use symbolism just like dreams. Often, at the initial stage, when you begin to receive this communication from God, you may not understand it. It may not come with interpretation. Or your spiritual senses may not be as developed to understand it or connect the dots. Do not panic. This would not stop communication from flowing to you. The Lord knows that it would take some time for you to catch up. He accounts for this. In this scenario, you may use the steps below for understanding.

Interpreting a Closed Vision

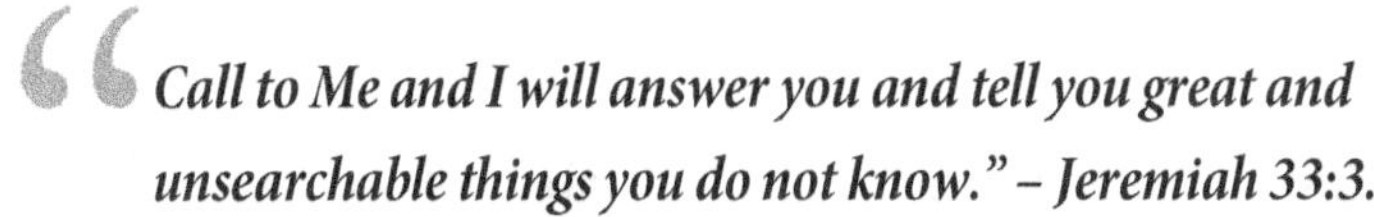

Call to Me and I will answer you and tell you great and unsearchable things you do not know." – Jeremiah 33:3.

1. Trust Your First Spiritual Impression - In order to train your spirit in accurate interpretation of a closed vision, usually and often, the first understanding that comes to your heart after the vision is the most accurate interpretation. Think of this like doing a Google search. The most likely answer to your query will be on the first page ranked at the top.

2. Ask The Lord For Clarity - If the answer is still not obvious, ask the Lord for interpretation.

3. Compare With Scripture – A closed vision will never contradict God's Word. Look for biblical parallels.

4. Consider The Context - In God's communication to you in a closed vision, the context of what is going in your life matters. If you are praying to the Lord on a particular issue, and while in prayers you see a closed vision, most of the time, the closed vision is answering your request. The closed vision in that case should be associated with your prayers. However, sometimes, you could also have a closed vision as an answer to your prayers long after you've prayed.

5. Interpret from the Known - God often speaks using things you already understand. He won't send you into confusion. Paul knew Macedonia was a city in Northern Greece, and top of his mind was preaching the gospel. This knowledge enabled Paul and his team to decide to leave for Macedonia at once. They concluded that God was calling them to preach the gospel there. In my example, I also concluded that God wanted me to reach out to my colleague for her salvation.

BIBLICAL EXAMPLE – Saul's Closed Vision

> *I have shown him a vision of a man named Ananias..."*
> — *Acts 9:12*

A clear example of a closed vision occurred when Saul encountered Jesus on the road to Damascus. After losing his sight, Saul spent three days in prayer and fasting, completely blind. During this time, God gave him a closed vision, revealing that a man named Ananias would come and restore his sight. Saul's physical eyes were shut due to blindness, but his spiritual eyes were open to see the vision of his coming healing. This prepared him to receive Ananias with faith, knowing his sight would be restored.

REAL LIFE RESULT – A Divine Answer Through a Closed Vision

There was a time when we were in financial need. My oldest daughter, the first in our family to attend college, was preparing to study out of state. She had been blessed with a full tuition scholarship, but here's the challenge: it didn't cover room and board, which amounted to about $13,000 per year. Taking out a loan wasn't an option for us—my wife and I were still paying off our own student loans. So, we waited, praying and hoping for good news about a highly competitive scholarship that could help cover the rest. But the announcement kept getting delayed.

As the days passed with no updates from the institution, my wife became increasingly anxious. "How are we going to bridge this financial gap?" she asked.

I have a routine of waking up before dawn to spend time with God in worship, prayer, and Bible reading. One morning, around 2 a.m., when the house was quiet and everyone else was asleep, I got up and went downstairs for my usual devotional time.

While praying with my eyes closed, I experienced a closed vision. I saw my daughter showing me her phone, filled with scholarship notifications. I was filled with joy. To me, it was a divine assurance that God had answered our prayers and would meet our financial need.

Later that afternoon, my daughter came to me, her face glowing with excitement. She shared the news that several scholarships had just been awarded to her. When she began her first semester, she owed nothing.

How to Position Yourself to Hear God Through Closed Visions

1. During Prayer

When you pray, you are engaging in direct communication with God. As you pour out your heart to Him, He may respond by showing you a vision in your mind's eye. For example, you might be praying about a decision such as whether to take a new job, move cities, or enter a new season in life. While praying, a sudden image appears: a bright open door, a path leading forward, or a specific place you've never thought of before. This is God communicating His answer visually, rather than speaking audibly or through an inner impression. The key sign that this is a closed vision is that you weren't imagining it, forcing it, or trying to see something. It simply appeared unexpectedly.

2. During Worship

Sometimes, when you are deeply engaged in worship, singing, praising, focusing on God's presence, you enter a spiritual atmosphere where God may reveal something to you visually. For example, as you close your eyes and lift your hands in worship, you may suddenly see a radiant light, an outstretched hand reaching toward you, or a symbolic image that feels deeply significant. Many people experience closed visions during worship because their hearts are fully turned toward God, making them sensitive to His voice.

When worship becomes wholehearted, heaven may respond with a vision.

3. During Bible Study

Have you ever read a verse in the Bible, and while reflecting on it with your eyes closed, a visual image appears in your mind? Something that clarifies or deepens the meaning? This could be a closed vision from God, helping you understand Scripture in a fresh and personal way. He often uses closed visions to make spiritual truths come alive in ways that teaching alone cannot accomplish.

Some scriptures aren't just read—they're seen with spiritual eyes.

4. During Daily Life

While closed visions most commonly occur during prayer or worship, God may sometimes show you something unexpectedly, even in everyday moments. For example, imagine sitting quietly in a café, reflecting on a challenge you're facing and suddenly, a clear image appears in your mind's eye, providing encouragement or direction. Perhaps you see a bridge leading across a river, symbolizing a path forward in your situation. Or maybe, a specific person's face appears, prompting you to reach out to them. Closed visions can come at moments when God wants to speak, even when you're not actively seeking Him.

God doesn't need a sacred setting to give you a sacred vision.

Best Practices for Discernment

- **Read and meditate on scripture regularly** – God's Word sharpens your spiritual perception.
- **Pray and ask** – Ask the Lord often in prayers to open your spiritual eyes.
- **Fast regularly** – Fasting heightens your spiritual awareness. **Seek confirmation** – Through peace, scripture, or godly counsel.
- **Write it down** – Details matter. Recording it ensures you don't forget key elements.
- **Don't rush decisions** – Let clarity settle.

Reflective Bridge

Has God already been speaking to you through closed visions, but you didn't realize it? God often answers the prayers you whisper with images you didn't expect. God still speaks and He wants you to recognize it and hear Him.

Encouragement

If you ever experience a closed vision, don't ignore it. Seek God for its meaning, and trust that He is guiding you toward truth. God is not silent. He is not distant. And He is not random.

I have shown him a vision…" – Acts 9:12

Reflection Questions

- Have I experienced this method before but missed the message?
- How can I cultivate more sensitivity to God's voice through closed visions?
- What steps can I take to better interpret what I see spiritually?

Closing Prayer

"Lord, by Your Holy Spirit, give me the gift of visions. Enable me to understand closed visions that you may be showing me. Empower me to act in faith. In Jesus' name, Amen."

CHAPTER 8

Hearing God Through Open Visions

"Then, after doing all those things, I will pour out My Spirit upon all people. Your sons and daughters will prophesy. Your old men will dream dreams, and your young men will see visions."

– JOEL 2:28

Picture yourself in a familiar setting. Maybe sitting in a quiet room, standing in prayer, or simply going about your day. Then suddenly, you see something. Not physically, but vividly before your eyes. A picture, a scene, an image that wasn't there just moments ago.

Your heart races. You blink, trying to understand what just happened. Yet, there's no denying it. God has just opened your eyes to the unseen.

One of the most powerful ways God speaks is through **open visions.** Moments when He reveals something beyond the natural realm while you are fully awake.

If you've ever had a sudden, unexplained vision that felt significant, don't dismiss it. It could be God revealing something directly to you.

What if that flash before your eyes wasn't your imagination—but an invitation from God?

What Is an Open Vision?

An **open vision** is a supernatural image, scene, or event that appears while your physical eyes are open, and you are fully awake. It's not a daydream. It's not symbolic imagination. Open visions allow you to see both the natural and supernatural simultaneously.

Open visions differ from:

- **Dreams** – Which happen during sleep.
- **Trances** – Which involve a deep stillness or sleep-like state.
- **Closed visions** – Which happen with your eyes shut.

Not everything you see is natural. Some things are supernatural.

Why Does God Speak Through Open Visions?

- To Warn and Protect – God may show you something critical. It could be a danger, a deception, a threat so you can act.
- To Direct or Instruct – An open vision might reveal a person to speak to, a step to take, or a place to go.
- To Reveal – These visions expose what's hidden, making the unseen obvious.
- To Answer Prayer - You may not hear words, but you'll see answers. Granting an answer to your prayer.

God's visions are not random. They're divine appointments.

How God Might Speak to You Through Open Visions

God's communication through visions, regardless of the type would always either be direct or symbolic. See the explanations on Closed Visions. In addition, below are specific to open vision.

1. Physical Eyes Vision

One of the ways God speaks in an open vision is what I call physical eyes vision. You see a supernatural event happening right in front of you, with your physical surroundings still visible. You may also start seeing what was invisible, suddenly becoming visible. E.g. Activity of angels. You are seeing another dimension at the same time with your physical eyes. You are seeing both simultaneously

2. Superimposed Vision

Another way that open vision works is when God overlays a picture, image, or scene onto what you are currently looking at, and allowing both the vision and reality to coexist. God may place a divine message over what you are currently looking at, like a picture-in-picture effect. You may still see your surroundings, but the focus is on the vision overlaying it, showing something, God wants you to notice.

God may superimpose His truth on top of your reality.

3. Mind's Eye Vision (While Awake)

This is when instead of appearing externally, an image or moving scene flashes suddenly in your mind while your eyes are open. It could be like a mental picture, but it is distinct and unplanned.

BIBLICAL EXAMPLE – Amos's Open Visions

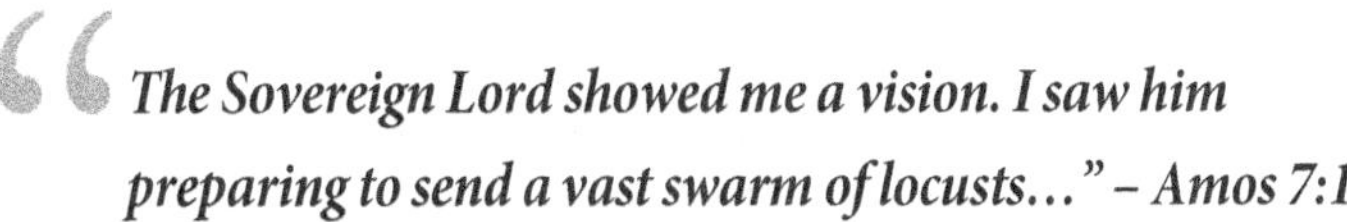

> *The Sovereign Lord showed me a vision. I saw him preparing to send a vast swarm of locusts…" – Amos 7:1*

Amos saw a vivid warning of impending destruction. Though awake, he saw it in real-time, so clearly that he pleaded for mercy and God responded.

REAL LIFE RESULT - When an Open Vision Brought Breakthrough

A while ago, I needed money for a project. I had tried everything I could to raise funds, but nothing seemed to be enough. So, I prayed and kept thinking about possible solutions.

Then, one Sunday evening, something unexpected happened. I was sitting on the bed, having a casual conversation with my wife, not praying, not expecting any revelation. But suddenly, something flashed before my eyes.

Even though I was fully awake, talking to my wife, I was interrupted by a vision. I saw a raw beef patty, like the ones sold in grocery stores for making burgers. It was so clear that I had to pause and signal to my wife to give me a moment to process what had just happened.

As I reflected on it, I began to ask God what this meant. My spirit, connected to the Holy Spirit, started searching deeper, almost like a spiritual Google search. And it landed on the company Beyond Meat.

I asked God for more understanding, and the message became clear: Invest in Beyond Meat's stock. Use what little money I had to grow the funds I had been praying for.

I obeyed, bought the stock, and within seven days, I saw over 100% profit. I sold the stock and used the money for my project.

The only regret I had? I wished I had trusted God more and invested even more than I did.

God speaks through visions, even about finances. If you've been asking Him for guidance, pay attention. His answer may come as a vision, an idea, or an unexpected thought that leads to breakthroughs.

The vision came without warning, but the blessing came with clarity.

How to Position Yourself to Hear God Through Open Visions

See the recommendations on Closed Visions.

Best Practices for Discernment

- **Ask for Clarity** – God interprets what He initiates.
- **Compare with Scripture** – The Word is your filter.
- **Interpret in Context** – Consider what was happening when the vision came.
- **Start from the Known** – God speaks through what you understand.
- **Seek Confirmation** – Peace, Scripture, or wise counsel will align.

Reflective Bridge

Has God already shown you an open vision, but you thought it was just a thought? Maybe you weren't imagining. Maybe you were encountering.

Encouragement

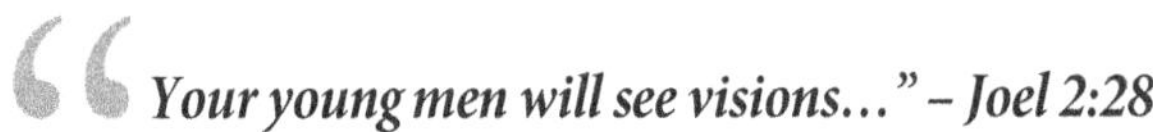

Your young men will see visions…" – Joel 2:28

God is revealing things to His children, often in ways we least expect. One of the major ways is through open visions. If you ever experience an open vision, don't ignore it. Seek God for its meaning, and trust that He is guiding you toward truth.

Reflection Questions

- Have I had an open vision and not realized its meaning?
- What can I do to become more spiritually aware and discerning?
- Am I willing to act when God shows me something?

Closing Prayer

"Lord, You promised to pour out Your Holy Spirit on me. Now I ask that You open my eyes to see visions according to Your promise. Help me to recognize Your voice, understand Your messages, and follow Your guidance with faith. In Jesus' name, Amen."

CHAPTER 9

Hearing God Through Night Visions

"For God speaks again and again, though people do not recognize it. He speaks in dreams, in visions of the night, when deep sleep falls on people as they lie in their beds."

– JOB 33:14–15 (NLT)

What if your final thought before sleep, or first one after wasn't yours, but God's?

Imagine you're lying in bed, eyes closed, slowly drifting into sleep. Your mind is quiet, your body relaxed. Then suddenly you see something. A picture, a moving scene, an image flashing before your eyes. It's clear, vivid, and it stirs something in your heart.

This isn't a dream. You're not imagining it. Could it be that God is speaking to you through a night vision?

Throughout the Bible, God has spoken to people in the stillness of the night—giving them direction, warnings, and insight when they were on the edge of sleep. He still speaks this way today. If you've ever had a vision before falling asleep or right after waking up, don't ignore it. It may be more than just a passing thought—it could be a divine message waiting to be understood.

What Is a Night Vision?

A night vision is a revelation from God such as a picture, sound, or event shown to you while you are half-awake or half-asleep. Unlike dreams (which occur in deep sleep), night visions happen when your mind is still semi-conscious. God speaks to you **before sleep takes over or before full wakefulness return. They are spiritual downloads with purpose.

God often waits for silence to speak clearly.

Why Does God Speak Through Night Visions?

1. Priority - God uses night visions to communicate urgent messages.
2. Busyness of the Day - If your mind has been occupied all day, God may wait until your spirit is quiet to speak.
3. Avoid Forgetfulness - God may give you visions of the night, so you don't forget what He is saying. Showing you something before sleep or right before waking, ensures you won't overlook it.
4. Answer to Prayers - God may give you a night vision as confirmation that your prayers have been answered. That means the Lord has completed all that is needed in the fulfillment of your request.

Some answers come after your prayer but before your morning.

How God Might Speak to You Through Night Visions

God's communication through visions, regardless of the type would always either be direct or symbolic. See the explanations on Closed Visions. In addition, the following are specific to night vision.

1. Just Before Falling Asleep

You may receive a night vision just before you fall into deep sleep. You lie in bed, the weight of the day slowly fading as sleep begins to pull you in.

Your thoughts drift, your body relaxes, and just as you approach to crossover into deep sleep, before your thoughts fully fade, God introduces a night vision. You may see a picture flash before your eyes, an event unfolding, hear a message, or suddenly understand something in your spirit before fully falling asleep.

2. Just Before Waking Up

You may also receive a night vision just before you are fully awake. As you're slowly coming back to awareness, still resting, still barely awake, a vision appears right before you fully open your eyes. This divine interruption happens before you get distracted by the day, ensuring you don't forget the message God is showing you.

BIBLICAL EXAMPLE – Paul's Night Vision

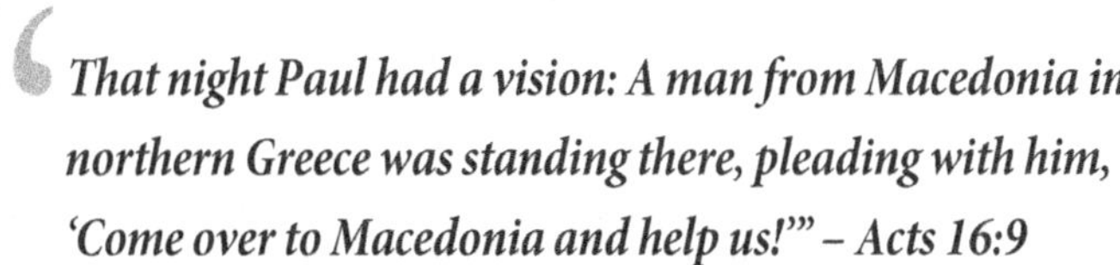

> *That night Paul had a vision: A man from Macedonia in northern Greece was standing there, pleading with him, 'Come over to Macedonia and help us!'" – Acts 16:9*

The bible is filled with many individuals who had night visions. Paul was one of such. He had plans to preach the gospel in Asia and Bithynia, but for some reason, which He didn't tell them, the Holy Spirit kept blocking them. And He didn't tell them where to go next (Acts 16:6-7).

This could also happen to you as well. You may have a good intention that is not the perfect will of God. The only reason you may know it's not God's perfect will might be the frustration from repeated failures.

Then, in a night vision, Paul saw a man from Macedonia calling for help. This was God's way of revealing Paul's next step: through a night vision, before full wakefulness clouded the message.

> *That night Paul had a vision: A man from Macedonia in northern Greece was standing there, pleading with him, 'Come over to Macedonia and help us!' So we decided to leave for Macedonia at once, having concluded that God was calling us to preach the Good News there." – Acts 16:9-10.*

REAL LIFE RESULT – A Night Vision That Led to Salvation

For years, I had a coworker I tried to share Christ with. I invited her to events, gave her devotionals, and had spiritual conversation, but nothing ever seemed to move her heart.

But then, something incredible happened! One Sunday morning at dawn, I had a night vision. In the vision, the Lord revealed personal details about her and her husband, including his name, which I had never known before. I rehearsed the details of the vision in my head to ensure that I did not forget it.

Knowing God had given me a divine message; I woke up excited. I reached for my phone and navigated to where I record my dreams and revelations, knowing this moment was far too significant to ignore.

The next day at work, I couldn't wait to reach out to her. I sent her an email, asking if we could meet up. We had some trouble finding a good time, but eventually, we settled on a Friday. When that Friday came, we met at the cafeteria in my office building. She was already there waiting for me, and we found a quiet spot away from the noisy crowd. After saying hello and catching up a bit, I got straight to the point. I told her why I wanted to see her.

I asked her a simple question: "Do you call your husband Bob?" She paused. Her face froze in shock.

"Yes! His full name is Robert, but I call him Bob. How did you know?" I smiled. *"Jesus told me."*

I explained to her that Jesus knows her and cares about her deeply. I talked to her some more about having a personal relationship with Jesus Christ.

Right there, in the middle of our office cafeteria, she gave her life to Jesus.

A single night vision can complete years of sowing.

How to Position Yourself to Receive Night Visions

- **Be spiritually attentive at night** – Don't fall asleep distracted. Wind down in prayer or worship.
- **Read scripture before bed** – Let God's Word set the tone.
- **Pray for vision** – Ask God specifically to speak.
- **Keep a journal by your bed** – Be ready to record what He shows you.
- **Fast occasionally** – Spiritual sensitivity sharpens in consecration.

8. Best Practices for Discernment

- **Ask God for Clarity** – If it came from Him, He'll explain it.
- **Compare with Scripture** – Truth never contradicts truth.
- **Interpret in Context** – What was happening in your life at the time?
- **Interpret from the Known** – God often uses familiar things.
- **Seek Confirmation** – Through scripture, peace, or godly counsel.

Reflective Bridge

Has God ever spoken just as you were falling asleep or waking up, but you brushed it off? God gives night visions to be understood not ignored. Your spirit can stay alert even when your body sleeps.

Encouragement

> *He speaks in dreams, in visions of the night…" – Job 33:15*

The quiet moments between sleep and waking are sacred. Don't dismiss them. Lean in. Ask. Record. Obey. God speaks in the night—and He's still speaking now.

God still speaks. And He wants you to hear. Even in the night.

Reflection Questions

- Have I dismissed a night vision, thinking it was just a thought or dream?
- What can I do to better position myself to hear God before I sleep or as I wake?
- How has God used night visions to answer my prayers or give direction?

Closing Prayer

"Lord, open my spiritual eyes. Give me the gift of seeing eyes. Give me the understanding of visions that You may be showing me. In Jesus' name, Amen."

CHAPTER 10

Hearing God Through Trances

"The next day as Cornelius's messengers were nearing the town, Peter went up on the flat roof to pray. It was about noon, and he was hungry. But while a meal was being prepared, he fell into a trance."

– ACTS 10:9–10

You're sitting in a quiet room, in a crowd, or maybe lost in thought or in conversation with someone. Then, suddenly, it happens. Your surroundings blur. Time seems to pause. You enter a momentary, sleep-like state. You see something. You hear something. You sense something beyond your surroundings. Then, as suddenly as it came, it's gone.

You blink. You refocus. What was that? You weren't dreaming. You weren't imagining it. It wasn't just a wandering thought. Could it be that **God was speaking through a trance?**

God speaks in many ways, and one of the most unexpected yet powerful ways is through trances—a moment where heaven interrupts earth with an urgent message.

God doesn't always whisper. Sometimes, He stops everything to speak.

What Is a Trance?

A **trance** is a sudden, God-induced state where you are fully awake one moment and then momentarily immersed in a spiritual encounter the next. You are not unconscious—but you are disconnected from the present. During a trance, God may show you a vision, speak a message, or give you divine instruction.

Unlike dreams (which happen during sleep), or closed visions (which happen with eyes shut), trances occur suddenly and while awake. It is always said that a person "falls into a trance" because it is never preplanned. And it may last for a few seconds or longer, but no matter how short, the message carries deep significance.

Why Does God Speak Through Trances?

God may speak through trances to you because some of His messages for you are too urgent to wait. Instead of speaking through dreams (which require you to sleep) or inner witness (which is a quiet leading), God may send a trance. He interrupts your conscious state to deliver an immediate revelation. Below are additional reasons:

For Urgency
Some messages can't wait until nightfall or prayer. God stops your world to deliver them.

For Revelation
He may need to show you something you could never perceive with natural senses.

For Redirection
You may be on the wrong path. Trances can instantly course correct.

For Deliverance or Healing
God may reveal hidden causes of pain or bondage so freedom can come.

Even a few seconds in a trance can carry years of breakthrough.

How God Might Speak to You Through a Trance

God's communication through trances also mimics that of visions. It would always either be direct or symbolic. See the explanations on Closed Visions. In addition, below are specific to trances

- You may see images, scenes, or spiritual events unfolding.
- You may hear specific instructions, warnings, or divine words.
- You may feel completely disconnected from the present moment until it's over.
- When the trance ends, you're fully awake again, but left with a message that demands reflection.

God doesn't need a long moment to make a lasting impact.

BIBLICAL EXAMPLE – Peter's Trance in Acts 10

> *He fell into a trance. He saw the sky open, and something like a large sheet was let down by its four corners..."*
> *– Acts 10:10–11*

One of the most well-known biblical trances happened to Apostle Peter. While praying, he suddenly fell into a trance, and in it, he saw a large sheet coming down from heaven, filled with animals that Jewish law considered "unclean."

Then, a voice spoke:

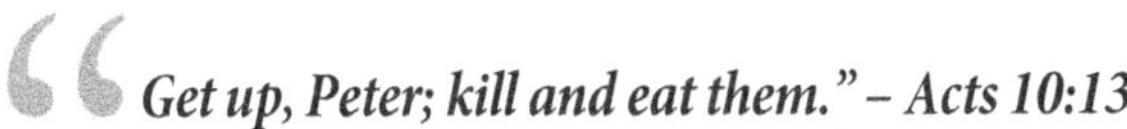

> *Get up, Peter; kill and eat them." – Acts 10:13*

Peter was puzzled. The command didn't make sense to him. Why would God ask him to eat something forbidden? But before he could understand, the Holy Spirit gave him another instruction **telling him that men were waiting downstairs for him.

Later, as events unfolded, Peter realized the trance wasn't about food. It was about people. God was showing him that salvation was not just for Jews but for Gentiles too.

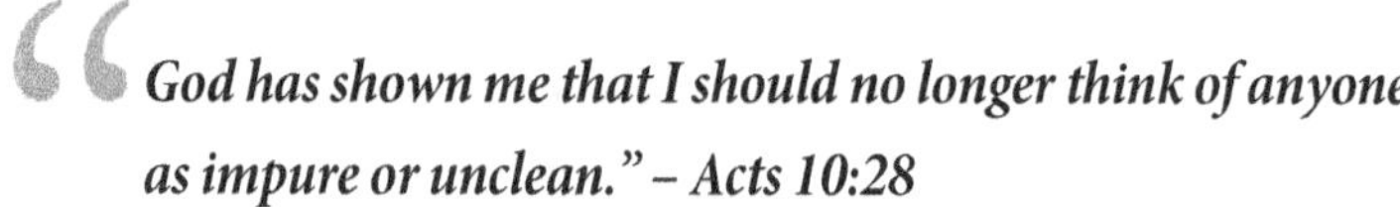

God has shown me that I should no longer think of anyone as impure or unclean." – Acts 10:28

REAL LIFE RESULT - When a Trance Led to Healing

I'll never forget the Saturday afternoon when God spoke in an unexpected way. I had just come back from a meeting, nothing unusual about the day. I sat down on my sofa to relax, and suddenly, I fell into a trance.

In that moment, I saw a woman I knew, and then, I heard the Lord whisper in my ear:

"She bedwets."

I was stunned. She was married. She had children. How was this possible? For a moment, I wondered. But deep down, I knew this wasn't random. Still, even if it was true, how could I approach her about such a personal issue?

Eventually, I reached out to her carefully, gently. She was shocked. She had been struggling with this since childhood and had prayed for healing for years. But she didn't know how to share her burden with others.

Through that trance, God revealed what had been hidden and provided an opportunity for prayer and deliverance. She was prayed for and she was healed.

Had I ignored the trance or hesitated in sharing it, I would have denied her the breakthrough God had prepared.

How to Position Yourself to Experience Trances

Trance is one of the revelatory (revealing) gifts of the Holy Spirit. Revelatory gifts are the gifts of the Holy Spirit that reveal hidden things, natural or supernatural. Therefore, it is the Holy Spirit who determines whether you experience a trance or not. However, you can do some things to trigger the operation of revelatory gifts in your life..

- **Be grounded in Scripture** – Truth anchors revelation.
- **Pray often** – Stay in ongoing dialogue with God.
- **Fast regularly** – Sharpen your spirit by quieting the flesh.
- **Live alert** – Expect that God may interrupt at any time.
- **Cultivate reverence** – Honor even the smallest spiritual impressions.

God chooses when but you can be ready.

8. Best Practices for Discernment

- **Guard What You See** – Be careful what you watch so you don't pollute your spiritual sight.
- **Pray For Discerning of Spirits** - Gift of discerning of spirits tells you what spirit is at work in a trance.
- **Pray For Interpretation** – Ask the Holy Spirit for interpretation.
- **Interpret from the Known** – God speaks through familiar things.
- **Seek Confirmation** – Look for peace, scripture, or counsel to affirm it.

Revelation is invitation. Discernment gives you direction.

Reflective Bridge

Has God ever stopped you in your tracks to show you something and you brushed it off? Perhaps you never recognized trances as was my experience too initially. Now you can stop guessing and begin recognizing. Lean in, seek understanding, and obey.

Encouragement

He fell into a trance…" – Acts 10:10

Peter wasn't seeking a trance. He was just hungry and praying. But God had something urgent to say. And He still does. Trust that He will speak to you.

Reflection Questions

- Have I ever experienced a trance without realizing its purpose?
- How can I prepare my spirit for unexpected divine interruptions?
- What steps can I take to grow in discernment regarding divine revelations?

Closing Prayer

"Lord, fill me with Your revelatory gifts. Let me not be in the dark spiritually. Give me wisdom to discern Your messages, the courage to act, and the patience to seek understanding. In Jesus' name, Amen."

CHAPTER 11

Hearing the Voice of God Through Inner Witness

"The Spirit Himself testifies with our spirit that we are God's children."

– ROMANS 8:16 (NIV)

It wasn't a loud voice. It wasn't a sign from heaven. But deep down, you felt a certainty, a quiet assurance that this was right.

Have you ever just known something deep in your spirit without explanation or logic? It wasn't a dream. It wasn't a sign. It was simply a quiet confidence… a sense that *this is right*. That subtle but steady sense of knowing is known as the **inner witness**. It is one of the clearest, most personal ways God speaks. As a believer, you have access to this supernatural guidance. It is a direct connection between your spirit and God's Spirit.

God may not shout—but He always confirms.

What Is the Inner Witness?

The **inner witness** is a supernatural knowing. It's not an emotion. It's not a guess. It's not human intuition. Unlike visions, dreams or trances, the inner witness doesn't come with visuals or voices. It's the Spirit of God communicating directly with your spirit, guiding you without needing words.

> *But you have an anointing from the Holy One, and all of you know the truth." – 1 John 2:20 (NIV)*

This is one of the ways God speaks and leads His children daily. No thunder. No dreams. Just conviction and supernatural knowing.

The Spirit within you knows what the mind cannot explain.

How God May Speak To You Through Inner Witness

A Deep "Yes" or "No" in Your Spirit

Have you ever faced a decision and just... knew what to do? It wasn't based on logic. It wasn't a gut feeling. It was a deep certainty in your spirit. That's God's inner witness confirming His direction.

> *Your own ears will hear him. Right behind you a voice will say, 'This is the way you should go.'" – Isaiah 30:21 (NLT)*

If you sense peace, proceed. But if there's uneasiness, hesitation, or discomfort, pause because God may be warning you.

A Quiet Conviction That Won't Go Away

Have you ever felt persistent conviction about something, maybe an action, a relationship, or a life decision? Even when you try to ignore it, it lingers, gently pressing on your heart. That's God's Spirit speaking, urging you toward righteousness. It's not guilt. It's **conviction.** Conviction isn't condemnation. It's God's love protecting you from deception and regret.

> *When He, the Spirit of truth, comes, He will guide you into all truth." – John 16:13*

A Supernatural Confidence That Defies Fear

Sometimes, God may lead you into unknown territory such as new job, a bold decision, a major shift. Logically, it may seem uncertain. Fear may whisper doubts. But despite the uncertainty, deep in your spirit, you feel sure. That confidence isn't arrogance. It's God's inner witness affirming His direction.

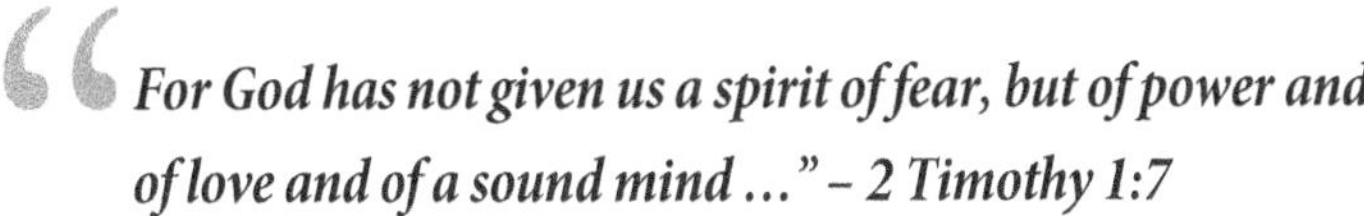

> *For God has not given us a spirit of fear, but of power and of love and of a sound mind …" – 2 Timothy 1:7*

When your heart says go but your head says wait, listen to the Spirit.

BIBLICAL EXAMPLE - Paul's Inner Witness: When God Guides from Within

One powerful example of God leading someone through an inner witness is Paul in Acts 16:6-10.

As Paul and his companions traveled, they planned to go to Asia to preach, but something felt off. They sensed that the Holy Spirit was stopping them. They tried again, heading toward Bithynia, but once more, they felt led not to go.

Then one night, Paul had a night vision. A man from Macedonia calling for help. After waking up, they felt a strong inner confirmation that Macedonia was where God wanted them to go.

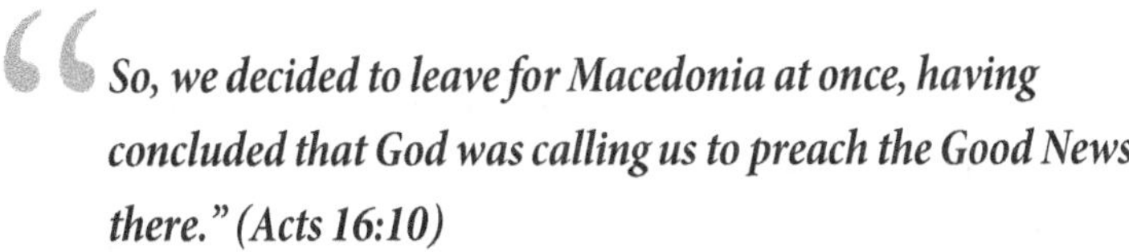

> *So, we decided to leave for Macedonia at once, having concluded that God was calling us to preach the Good News there." (Acts 16:10)*

It was a combination of a vision and an inner witness, a deep knowing in their spirit that guided their decision.

Paul's story shows that sometimes, God speaks through a strong inner sense of direction, even before external confirmation comes

REAL LIFE RESULT - When the Inner Witness Led Me in the Right Direction

I remember a decision that, on paper, seemed all wrong. The timing wasn't great. The resources weren't ideal. When I discussed it with those around me, they were fearful. They almost swayed me to their side with their trepidation. But every time I prayed, I felt the knowing that it was going to be okay.

So, I decided to move forward. And as I moved forward, everything aligned perfectly. Confirming that the inner witness was God's leading all along.

Have you ever felt something similar? That deep certainty before your mind caught up? That's God speaking through His Spirit.

Inner witness is sometimes the loudest confirmation God gives.

How to Position Yourself to Hear the Inner Witness

- **Create quiet space** – The inner witness may be easily drowned out by noise.
- **Stay in God's Word** – Develop a closer relation with the Scripture to tune your heart to truth.
- **Pray about everything** – Don't wait for crisis. Include God in every step.
- **Obey the small nudges** – Faithfulness in small impressions builds trust for bigger ones.
- **Check for peace** – God's Spirit speaks most often through inner rest or restraint.

A sensitive spirit hears what a busy soul misses.

Best Practices for Discernment

- Compare with Scripture – God's Spirit never contradicts His Word.
- Watch for consistency – The inner witness stays steady, not emotional.
- Get wise counsel – God can confirm through mature believers. Pray frequently – Praying often allows you to be in the spirit always.
- Test it in prayer – Ask God to affirm or adjust your sense.

If it's truly from God, it will stand under prayer and Scripture.

Reflective Bridge

Has God been trying to guide you quietly, but you've been waiting for something louder? You are not sure if it's from God and guessed it was just overconfidence? Now you know it's God inner witness.

Encouragement

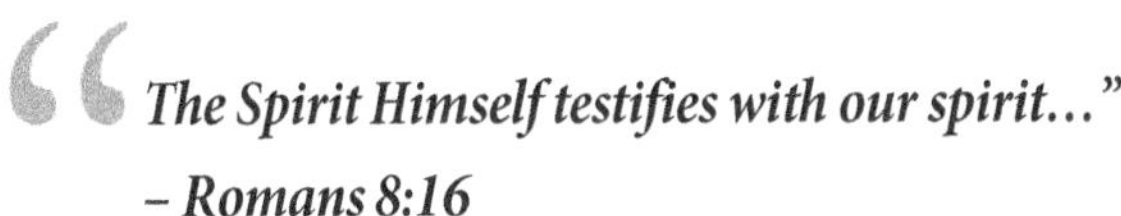

The Spirit Himself testifies with our spirit…"
– Romans 8:16

God's voice isn't always dramatic. Often, it's a whisper within a settled "yes," a holy hesitation, a consistent pull. Learn to trust it.

Reflection Questions

- Have I ever ignored an inner prompting and regretted it?
- What consistent impressions has God been giving me lately?
- How can I tune my heart to become more sensitive to His inner witness?

Closing Prayer

"Lord, help me recognize Your voice through Your Spirit's inner witness. Teach me to trust the quiet confirmations You give me. Make my heart sensitive to Your leading, and give me the courage to obey. In Jesus' name, Amen."

CHAPTER 12

Hearing God Through Perception

*"When the Spirit of truth comes,
He will guide you into all truth."*

– JOHN 16:13

You walk into a room, and before anyone says a word, you sense something is off. Nothing looks wrong, but deep inside, you just know. Or maybe you meet someone, and without any obvious reason, you feel there's more to their story. Something they haven't said.

That's **spiritual perception**. It's one of the quietest yet most powerful ways God speaks. It's how He nudges your heart without using words.

Perception isn't loud. It doesn't demand attention. But when you pay attention, it's real.

God's voice doesn't always sound. It sometimes feels.

What Is Perception?

Perception is a Spirit-led awareness. It is a way God makes something known to you, through sensing and understanding that is beyond words. God can guide your thoughts, feelings, or insights. It is a sense in your heart that comes from God, not from evidence, logic, or external cues. It's a form of inner discernment, **where the Holy Spirit reveals something directly to your spirit.**

It may come as a deep knowing, a sudden unease, or a gentle nudge that something is right or not.

In 2 Kings 4:9, a Shunammite woman sensed Elisha was a holy man of God. He never announced it. No miracles had been done. But **she perceived it in her spirit**.

Jesus affirmed this kind of spiritual awareness when He said:

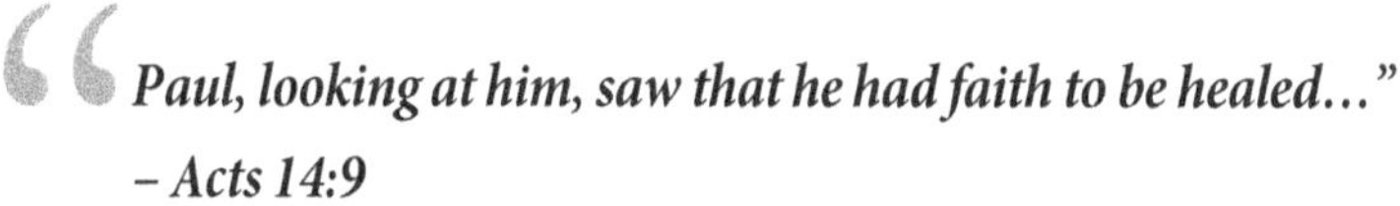

When the Spirit of truth comes, He will guide you into all truth." – John 16:13

How God May Speak To You Through Perception

1. A Sudden Feeling or Sensing

You may meet someone who looks fine, but you feel prompted to pray. Or you walk into a place and feel uneasiness, though nothing is visibly wrong. That's often God warning or inviting you to become spiritually alert.

Paul, looking at him, saw that he had faith to be healed…"
– Acts 14:9

In **Acts 14:9**, Paul looked at a man and perceived he had faith to be healed. This wasn't based on anything the man said. It was something Paul sensed deeply.

Spiritual perception often shows up before logic does.

2. A Warning or Sense of Danger

God sometimes gives perception as a form of protection. You may feel uneasy about a situation or decision, and later realize He was guiding you away from trouble. Others may not feel the same thing, but deep down, you know something is off. Paul experienced this in **Acts 19:21**, when he felt compelled by the Holy Spirit to change his journey.

> *Paul felt compelled by the Spirit…" – Acts 19:21*

Sometimes God protects you through what others can't see.

3. A Call to Action

Sometimes perception is an invitation to **do something**. To pray, to encourage, or to help. You may feel urged to pray for someone at a specific moment, even though they haven't asked for it. God may place a burden on your heart to reach out to someone in need.

> *The Spirit himself testifies with our spirit that we are God's children." – Romans 8:16*

If it presses on your heart without logic, it may be from God.

BIBLICAL EXAMPLE: Paul's Perception of Faith

In Acts 14:9, Paul was preaching in Lystra when he noticed a man in the crowd—someone who had been crippled since birth.

As Paul spoke, he sensed something about this man. Without hearing him say anything or seeing any obvious signs, **Paul perceived** that he had faith to be healed.

This wasn't based on words or actions. It was **spiritual perception**, a deep knowing that came from Paul's connection with God and the Holy Spirit.

With boldness, Paul looked at the man and said, "Stand up on your feet!" Immediately, the man jumped up and began to walk.

This moment shows how important spiritual sensitivity is. Paul didn't need proof. He simply recognized the faith in the man and responded.

It's a reminder for us today: God speaks in many ways, and if we stay close to Him, He can lead us, even through perception.

REAL LIFE RESULT – When Perception Opened the Door to Clarity

There was a time when I had a conversation with someone I knew. Outwardly, they were composed, cheerful, and polite. But as we spoke, I sensed something else. Weight beneath the surface. I couldn't explain it.

Later that night, the Lord confirmed in prayer that the person was in emotional distress. I reached out, asked a few gentle questions, and sure enough, **they opened up completely**.

What you perceive may be someone else's breakthrough waiting to happen.

How to Grow in Spiritual Perception

Perception is not guesswork. It's a spiritual muscle. And like all spiritual gifts, it grows with intentional practice.

- **Pray regularly for others – Intercessory prayer for others sharpens your sensitivity.**
- **Study the Bible** – Scripture reveals how God speaks and moves.

- **Journal promptings** – Notice the small nudges and reflect on how God guides you over time.
- **Act on gentle nudges** – If you feel led to pray for someone, do it. Acting on God's guidance makes perception stronger.
- **Ask for discernment** – James 1:5 promises God gives wisdom generously.

The more you respond, the clearer you perceive.

Best Practices for Discernment

- **Check with Scripture** – Perception will always align with God's Word.
- **Use Wisdom & Right Timing** – Filter every perception through wisdom and right timing.
- **Watch for consistency** – The Holy Spirit's promptings won't confuse.
- **Seek Clarity** – Even urgent perception will come with clarity, not panic.
- **Ask trusted believers** – God may confirm through counsel.

Perception must be filtered through wisdom, not assumption.

Reflective Bridge

Have you ever sensed something you couldn't explain, but were too unsure to act? When you first experience spiritual perception, it's easy to dismiss it as a random feeling. Does it repeat? Then it's not random. Recognize and accept it next time.

Maybe you didn't imagine it. Maybe you perceived it.

Encouragement

God doesn't only speak through words. **He speaks through awareness.** Spiritual perception is a sign of closeness with Him. As you stay in prayer, stay in Scripture, and stay sensitive, **you'll begin to recognize His movements more clearly.**

God still speaks. And sometimes, you just know.

Reflection Questions

- Have I ever sensed something spiritually without evidence—and it turned out to be true?
- What keeps me from trusting God's voice through perception?
- How can I grow more confident in acting on spiritual nudges?

Closing Prayer

"Lord, open my heart to perceive Your guidance. Help me trust Your voice and follow Your direction with confidence. Sharpen my spiritual awareness so that I may respond to Your leading with wisdom and obedience. Amen."

CHAPTER 13

Hearing The Voice of God Through Nature

"The heavens are telling of the glory of God; and their expanse is declaring the work of His hands. Day to day pours forth speech, and night to night reveals knowledge."

— PSALM 19:1-2 (NASB)

Not all of God's messages will come to you wrapped in words. Sometimes He paints them across the sky, sings them through the rustling of trees, or whispers through rushing waters. Creation itself becomes the canvas of God's voice. Do you know speaking through nature is one of the natural ways that God speaks? While looking for how to hear the voice of God, don't forget this method of communication right before you.

What Is Hearing God Through Nature?

This is when God uses His creation to communicate something specific to your heart. It might be a literal, direct message spoken to your spirit while observing nature. Nature becomes a mirror or metaphor for a truth God wants to highlight. He speaks through the beauty and stillness of His works, and He knows how to draw your attention. On the other hand, nature could also become the pathway for opening your spirit to access communication from God.

Not everything is from God—but God does speak this way.

Why Does God Speak Through Nature?

1. To Remind Us of His Glory

Nature reflects God's majesty and creative power. It stirs awe and invites you to look beyond yourself.

Psalm 19:1 shows how creation declares His glory.

2. To Quiet the Noise

In a busy, loud world, nature provides silence, and God often speaks in the stillness.

1 Kings 19:12 reminds us God was not in the earthquake, but in the whisper.

3. To Draw You into His Presence

Time in nature pulls you away from distractions and into wonder, aligning your heart to hear.

Psalm 23:2 says, "He leads me beside still waters. He restores my soul."

4. To Deliver Insight in Moments of Rest

There are many testimonies that involve people hearing from God while walking, gazing at the stars, or simply sitting under a tree.

How God Might Speak to You Through Nature

God can speak to through nature via Direct Communication or Pathway.

Direct Communication is when God speaks to you directly using nature. These may become metaphors or symbols.

1. Through Sunsets and Skies

You may sense God's peace or comfort through the colors of the evening sky. You are driving home after a long day at work. Then He chooses hues instead of words, painting the sky to gently whisper to your soul. Imagine a vast expanse of orange and gold pouring over the horizon, the sun dipping low as if bowing in reverence to the day. Each streak of crimson and violet seems like a brushstroke of love, a reminder of His presence and care. In those quiet, glowing moments, the fading light wraps around you like a warm embrace. You don't know how to describe but you can feel it that God is saying, "Be still; I am here. You are seen, you are loved, and tomorrow holds promise."

2. Through Trees, Leaves, and Wind

God may use trees, leaves and even the wind to speak to you especially if you are in a certain season in your life. For example, the way a tree sheds its leaves may speak to you about letting go, or a strong wind might symbolize a coming change.

Pathway is another major way that God communicates through nature. This is when nature becomes the portal **for opening your spirit to access communication from God.** This is similar to when worship music is used as a pathway to open your spirit to connect with God.

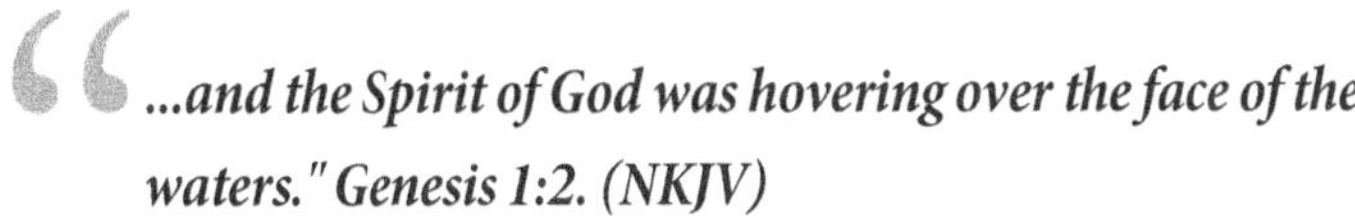

...and the Spirit of God was hovering over the face of the waters." Genesis 1:2. (NKJV)

3. By Water

Rivers, Lakes, Oceans, Seas

Many people report feeling a deeper connection to God when near large bodies of water, whether sitting beside a lake or walking along a beach. Have you ever experienced this? The Bible mentions several instances of God speaking to individuals by rivers or seas. For example, God revealed future events to Daniel by the Tigris River (Daniel 10) and spoke to Ezekiel by the Kebar River (Ezekiel 3:14). Moreover, the Spirit of God is described as hovering over the waters in Genesis, a powerful image of divine presence that resonates throughout Scripture.

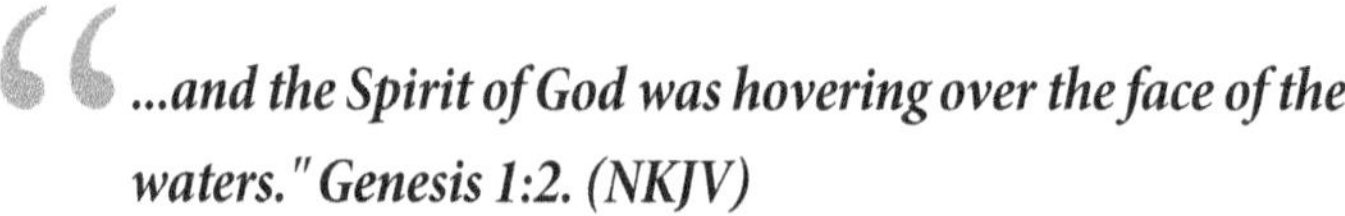

...and the Spirit of God was hovering over the face of the waters." Genesis 1:2. (NKJV)

Shower or Bath

Another portal for getting communication from God is while you are in the shower or when taking a bath. It could be early in the morning or late at night. The calming effect of water helps settle your mind and quiet your spirit, making it easier to perceive divine thoughts. Relax and pay attention to ideas, impressions, closed visions, and thoughts that come to you. You can further enhance this with worship music playing in the background.

He leads me beside still waters..." Psalm 23:2

4. During Walks or Hikes

Another pathway that can create the space for His impressions to rise within you are walks and hikes. It could happen in the quietness of your walk or hike. As you communicate with God during walks, He could place an impression in your heart.

God speaks best when we slow down enough to listen.

BIBLICAL EXAMPLE – Daniel at the River

In **Daniel 10:4–6**, Daniel was standing by the Tigris River when he has a life-altering vision. He sees a man clothed in linen with a belt of pure gold, whose appearance radiates divine majesty.

This wasn't random scenery. The river became the backdrop for a supernatural encounter. Daniel wasn't asleep; he wasn't seeking a vision. He was simply present and God chose that moment to speak.

This moment reveals a powerful truth: being in nature often opens a gateway to spiritual clarity.

REAL LIFE RESULT – When My Shower Became a Place of Revelation

I've learned to pay attention while taking a shower, because God often speaks to me there. Sometimes, He gives me ideas for my business or ministry and even reveals names of people who need help.

One of the most powerful moments happened years ago. As I stood under the water, God began to speak through my thoughts, telling me about the direction of my life. He revealed gifts He had placed inside me. Gifts I never knew I had.

At the time, I didn't fully understand. But now, years later, I've seen those gifts come to life, just as He said.

That shower became more than just a routine. It became a sacred space. Not because the water was special, but because God chose it as a channel to speak.

God can use ordinary moments to do extraordinary things if you stay open to Him

How to Position Yourself to Hear God Through Nature

- Start by paying attention to your ordinary routines such as bath/shower or walks.
- Schedule quiet moments outside—even 10 minutes of stillness.
- Ask God to make you aware of what He wants to show you.
- Look for repetition or beauty that seems to "stand out."
- Bring a journal. Write down impressions, questions, or peace you feel.
- Practice gratitude often. Thank God often for the beautiful things He has created.

Best Practices for Discernment

- **Test every message** against Scripture. God never contradicts Himself.
- **Journal regularly** to track patterns and confirmations.
- **Stay grounded** in prayer, fasting and biblical study.
- **Talk it out** with trusted spiritual mentors.
- **Make space for silence**—noise dulls your hearing.

Avoid idolizing nature or seeking mystical experiences. Creation is the vessel, not the source.

Reflective Bridge

That moment in the shower, when clarity comes out of nowhere, what if that wasn't just your mind wandering? What if it was God cutting through the noise to get to you? You're not guessing. You're being guided.

Encouragement

You don't have to climb a mountain or wait for a lightning bolt. If you slow down and listen, creation will begin to echo His whispers.

God is always speaking—sometimes through rivers and roots, skies and stillness.

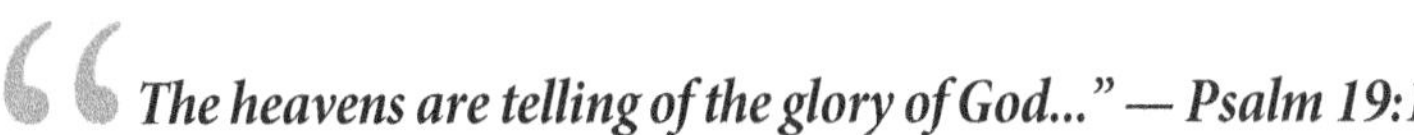 *The heavens are telling of the glory of God..." — Psalm 19:1*

Reflection Questions

1. When was the last time nature made you pause and reflect?
2. Have you experienced peace or insight during a walk, by water, or in a quiet moment?
3. What can you do this week to create space to hear God through His creation?

Closing Prayer

"Lord, open my eyes to see You in all You have made. Let the beauty of creation stir my spirit to hear Your voice. Teach me to listen in stillness, and respond with trust. Amen."

CHAPTER 14

Hearing God Through Your Thoughts

"² Don't copy the behavior and customs of this world, but let God transform you into a new person by changing the way you think. Then you will learn to know God's will for you, which is good and pleasing and perfect."

- Romans 12:2.

In my earlier stages of trying to hear the voice of God, I missed His voice because I was expecting the most profound messages from Him to present themselves in a very spectacular way. Then I discovered that the most consistent way that God speaks and leads us is not as with a loud voice booming from Mount Sinai like He did with Moses. Instead, His communication may present itself subtly as thoughts.

One moment you're doing something ordinary like folding laundry, driving to work, or brushing your teeth, and suddenly, a name flashes across your mind. Or a Bible verse you haven't read in months surfaces in your spirit. It doesn't feel like your own thought. It carries weight. It stays with you.

And then, confirmation comes. You reach out, and someone says, "I needed that." You read the verse, and it's exactly what you needed.

These aren't coincidences. These are divine impressions.

What if it was God speaking all along—right through your thoughts?

What Is Hearing God Through Your Thoughts?

This is when God uses **thought** impressions, implanted thoughts, or spontaneous insights to communicate with you. It's not an audible voice. It's not always emotional. But it brings **clarity, conviction, or revelation** that feels deeper than your natural thinking. God may plant a scripture, a name, an answer, or an idea directly in your mind. Not every thought is from God—but some absolutely are.

"For who has known the mind of the Lord so as to instruct him? But we have the mind of Christ." – 1 Corinthians 2:16

Not every thought is from God—but some absolutely are.

Why Does God Speak Through Thoughts?

1. To Deliver Guidance Swiftly

Thoughts are instant. When you need quick direction or encouragement, God may bypass the noise and send an impression directly to your mind.

2. To Reveal Truth Without Drama

Not every message from God needs a sign or miracle. Some of His clearest words come through still, quiet thoughts.

3. To Implant Divine Knowledge

There are moments when you suddenly "know" something you had no way of knowing. This is supernatural. This is the Holy Spirit.

> *But the Advocate, the Holy Spirit... will teach you all things..." – John 14:26*

4. To Solve Problems with Wisdom

God can also insert divine wisdom into your thoughts, giving you **strategies, solutions, or instructions** you didn't previously have.

How God Might Speak to You Through Thoughts

1. Thought Impressions

One way God speaks to His children is through thought impressions—spontaneous, persistent thoughts that linger, often prompting you to pray, reach out, or take action.

Have you experienced this before? Perhaps you're working, and an old friend's name suddenly comes to mind. You dismiss it as a random thought, but an hour later, it resurfaces. Then again. It won't leave your mind until you act on it. Finally, you call, only to discover they're in crisis.

That thought? It wasn't random or coincidence. It was God speaking to you. Because He uses the natural flow of your thoughts, it's easy to overlook. But when a thought keeps returning, pay attention.

Acts 10:19 – *While Peter was thinking about the vision, the Spirit said to him...*

2. Knowledge Implantation

God may also speak to you by implanting knowledge directly into your thoughts—giving you information you couldn't have known naturally. Suddenly, you know something without understanding how.

As humans, we typically gain knowledge through senses like sight and hearing, which our brains interpret. However, as the Creator, God can bypass these inputs and place knowledge directly within us. That's why you might say, *"I don't know how—I just knew."*

This knowledge can about you, others, or events, past, present, or future. It is one of the Holy Spirit's gifts, known as **Word of Knowledge (1 Corinthians 12:8)**.

3. Wisdom Implantation

Another way God may speak to you through your thoughts is by wisdom implantation. He gives you wisdom in a way that feels sudden and unexpected. This is called Word of Wisdom, a gift of the Holy Spirit (**1 Corinthians 12:8**). This is divine strategy. When God gives you a brilliant idea, the solution to a complex issue, or next steps that bring clarity.

Imagine facing a really difficult problem, one that seems impossible to fix. Then, out of nowhere, a solution appears in your mind. You didn't learn it or figure it out. It just came to you. You don't know *how* you know it, but you *do* know.

Scripture: James 1:5 – *"If any of you lacks wisdom, let him ask God..."*

You don't know how to fix a situation, but suddenly, a plan drops into your spirit. That's wisdom from above.

BIBLICAL EXAMPLE: Solomon's Implanted Wisdom

In 1 Kings 3:16–28, King Solomon faced a case where two women came before him, each claiming to be the mother of the same living child. There were no witnesses, no DNA tests, no way to verify who is telling the truth.

In that moment, Solomon received supernatural wisdom. He says, "Bring me a sword." The crowd must have gasped. He commanded the living child to be cut in two and shared between the women. It was not cruelty. It was divine insight.

Immediately, the real mother cries out in agony and begs the king to give the child to the other woman. She was willing to lose her son so he might live. Solomon instantly knew: this was the true mother.

This wasn't courtroom logic. It was heaven's wisdom implanted into Solomon's mind. There was no time for analysis. It was a thought from God that led to unmistakable clarity.

REAL LIFE RESULT- When God Planted Knowledge In My Spirit

One of my most memorable experiences with knowledge implantation happened during a prayer retreat.

Every year, my church holds a three-day retreat at Blue Mountain Christian Retreat Center in Pennsylvania. On Friday nights, an elder and I always set aside time for extra prayer. We used to pray in our rooms, but as our voices grew louder, we decided to move to the 24-hour chapel. It is a place where people from all over come to seek God.

One particular year, we arrived early, kneeling at the altar and pouring out our hearts in prayer. Over time, others entered quietly, praying silently. We stayed focused on God, barely noticing them—until something remarkable happened.

The Lord began implanting names and burdens into our thoughts, revealing details about those praying around us. At first, we hesitated, unsure if we should act. But the impressions were so clear and persistent that we finally turned to the others and gently asked, _"Is someone here named __?"

One by one, they confirmed. One of them, a woman with a painful leg condition, was healed instantly when we prayed for her.

This can happen to you too. If God places something in your thoughts, lean in. Ask. Don't let fear hold you back. If you're wrong, don't be discouraged. It's like learning to ride a bike. Keep going, keep listening, and trust that God is leading you.

How to Position Yourself to Hear God Through Thoughts

- **Spend time in the Word**—it trains your mind to think God's thoughts (Romans 12:2).
- **Be Sensitive To Your Thoughts**- While thoughts are natural to you, they are also pathways for divine communication.
- **Be Sensitive In Prayer** — While praying, don't lock up or shut down your thoughts.
- **Keep a journal**. Write down any thoughts or impressions that feel weighty.
- **Obey quickly when** thoughts persist with peace.

Don't assume every thought is divine. Test them.

Best Practices for Discernment

- **Test it with Scripture.** God's thoughts align with His Word (Romans 12:1-2.
- **Avoid A Judgmental Spirit.** A judgmental spirit would make you operate in the flesh.
- **Avoid fear-based impulses.** The Spirit leads by love and wisdom.

- **Avoid People Profiling.** Don't profile people and use this as God speaking.

Reflective Bridge

That gentle nudge... the idea that won't go away... the verse that randomly floated into your mind—what if it wasn't random at all? You may have been brushing off divine thoughts without knowing it—until now. You were never meant to guess.

Encouragement

God is not hiding His voice. He speaks in ways your spirit can grasp—and your thoughts are one of them.

You don't need a lightning bolt when a whisper will do.

You have the mind of Christ. And God is still speaking.

> *My sheep hear My voice, and I know them, and they follow Me." – John 10:27*

Callout: God still speaks. And He wants you to hear Him.

Reflection Questions

1. Have you ever had a thought that later turned out to be from God?
2. What holds you back from trusting impressions in your spirit?
3. How can you begin discerning God's voice more clearly through your thoughts?

Closing Prayer

"Lord, think through my thoughts. Let every thought that comes from You be confirmed with peace and truth. Quiet the noise within me so I may hear You clearly. I welcome Your wisdom and insight. In Jesus' name, Amen."

CHAPTER 15

Hearing the Voice of God Through Speaking in Tongues & Interpretation

"For if I pray in tongues, my spirit is praying, but I don't understand what I am saying."

– 1 CORINTHIANS 14:14

Ever wondered if God could speak to you in a language beyond your understanding?

Jesus promised that one of the signs accompanying believers would be the ability to speak in new languages or tongues (Mark 16:17). This gift, given by the Holy Spirit, isn't just about speaking. It's about hearing and receiving divine revelation through the interpretation of tongues.

Speaking in tongues is more than a spiritual practice. It is a supernatural channel for communication with God. But unless you understand what is being spoken, you could be missing out on deeper revelations.

Let's explore how God speaks through tongues and interpretation, and how you can step into this profound way of hearing His voice.

What Is Speaking in Tongues?

Speaking in tongues is the Spirit-enabled ability to communicate in a language not learned by the speaker. It is God's direct gift, given when a believer is baptized in the Holy Spirit (Acts 2:1-3). These languages can be:

- Earthly languages, unknown to the speaker but spoken by others
- Heavenly languages, understood only by God

Not everything spoken in tongues is for others to hear—but everything has a purpose in God.

Why Does God Speak Through Tongues?

1. To Strengthen the Believer

Tongues edify your spirit when your mind is weary (1 Corinthians 14:4).

2. To Enable Deep Communion

Tongues allow your spirit to pray when words fail you (Romans 8:26).

3. To Release Interpretation and Prophecy

Interpretation unlocks prophetic understanding hidden in tongues (1 Corinthians 12:10).

4. To Be a Sign for Unbelievers

Tongues demonstrate God's supernatural presence (Acts 2:7–11).

5. To Bypass Human Limitations (1 Corinthians 14:2:)

Tongues allow your spirit to bypass human limitations speaking mysteries straight to God. It's like speaking in a top-secret phone line that can't be hacked.

Types of Tongues

1. Known Earthly Language

The first type of tongues is a known human language, but unknown to the speaker.

Example: At Pentecost, when the Holy Spirit fell, people from different nations heard the disciples speaking in their own languages (Acts 2:7-11). The disciples had never studied those languages, yet God enabled them to speak as a sign to unbelievers.

Even today, God may empower someone to speak in another earthly language intended for someone who understands it.

2. Unknown Heavenly Language

A heavenly language is a spiritual dialect known only to God.

Paul describes this when he says:

*"For if I pray in tongues, my spirit is praying, but I don't understand what I am saying."*** – 1 Corinthians 14:14**

When you pray in heavenly tongues, your spirit is in direct communion with God. It bypasses your mind and engages your deepest spiritual core.

How God Might Speak to You Through Tongues

Speaking in tongues isn't just about uttering words. It is a gateway to divine revelation.

When you pray in tongues, God might:

- Instantly answer your prayer with direction or breakthrough.
- Deepen your spiritual insight and provide revelation beyond human words.

- Unveil prophetic instruction guiding you toward His will.
- Foretell events, offering warnings or encouragement

How Interpretation Works in Private Prayer

If praying in tongues privately by yourself, interpretation might come as you are speaking in tongues. As you are speaking, the interpretation of what you are saying will be relayed or transcribed in your heart/spirit. It could be via thought, phrase, or even the bringing of images together to produce the interpretation. If the interpretation is not vocalized, it sits in your spirit.

BIBLICAL EXAMPLE – Tongues and Interpretation in Action

"...the ability to interpret what is being said." I Corinthians 12:10. Paul describes interpretation as one of the nine gifts of the Holy Spirit (**1 Corinthians 12:10**).

Interpretation is not a direct, word-for-word translation. Rather, it reveals the meaning behind what is spoken in tongues.

REAL LIFE RESULT – When God Spoke to Me Through Tongues and Interpretation

When I was first baptized with the Holy Spirit, I began speaking in an unknown tongue. Initially, it was sporadic and slow, but over time, it became more frequent. Though I didn't understand the words I was saying, each moment felt spiritually energizing, and I experienced God's presence profoundly.

As I persisted, devoting more time to prayer, especially praying in tongues, something remarkable unfolded. Gradually, I began to receive interpretations of what I was saying. Sometimes, I would speak the interpretations aloud; other times, I quietly absorbed them, recording them when necessary.

A few years ago, during my morning prayers, something extraordinary happened. As I walked back and forth between the living room and the kitchen, praying as was my habit, I began speaking in tongues. Suddenly, the Holy Spirit provided an interpretation. It started as a deep, instinctive understanding within my spirit, which I then vocalized along the lines of:

"I am trying to hide you. Do not accept outside invitations. You are not ready."

Three weeks later, I was invited to preach at a convention, but I declined. For the next four years, I ministered solely within my local church, except for one emergency occasion when my leadership assigned me to deliver a virtual sermon for a congregation in transition. Aside from that, I turned down every other invitation to speak, teach, or preach.

If I hadn't embraced the ability to interpret the tongues I spoke, I might have inadvertently disobeyed God or exposed myself to unnecessary risks.

This gift is available to you, too. Press in. Believe. Exercise it.

How to Position Yourself to Hear God Through Tongues & Interpretation

If you want to **activate this gift**, here are steps you can take:

1. **Worship before you pray** – Invite God's presence through worship.
2. **Pray for the baptism of the Holy Spirit** – If you don't speak in tongues yet, ask God for this gift.
3. **Speak in tongues freely** – Let the Spirit lead you in utterance.
4. **Ask God for interpretation** – Expect insight to come.

5. **Pause after praying in tongues** – Listen and wait.
6. **Write down impressions** – Keep track of what God reveals.

Don't ignore or rush what you sense—wait and weigh it prayerfully.

Best Practices for Discernment

- Pray consistently in tongues—make it a daily practice.
- Be sensitive to thoughts, words, or scriptures that rise in your spirit.
- Trust the interpretation process—it will grow stronger over time.
- Share insights with a mentor —iron sharpens iron.
- Confirm through Scripture – God's words align with His truth.

Reflective Bridge

Could that phrase that rose in your spirit... that vision during tongues... that peace afterward... have been God all along? The supernatural doesn't always make sense. Don't be afraid of God's supernatural communication to you. Embrace it.

Encouragement

Hearing God through tongues and interpretation is one of the most intimate and powerful experiences a believer can have. It may feel unfamiliar at first, but as you practice and grow, you will recognize God's voice more clearly. God desires to speak to you in ways beyond human understanding. Don't be afraid to listen.

Reflection Questions

1. Have you ever received interpretation while praying in tongues?
2. What holds you back from listening for God's voice afterward?
3. How might you grow this gift intentionally?

Closing Prayer

"Lord, I long to hear Your voice through the language of the Spirit. Fill me with boldness to pray in tongues and humility to wait for understanding. Open my heart to interpretation. Speak clearly, Lord—I'm listening. In Jesus' name, Amen."

CHAPTER 16

Hearing God Through Others

*"Every matter must be established by the testimony of
two or three witnesses."*

– 2 CORINTHIANS 13:1

What if God has been speaking to you through the people around you, but you haven't noticed?

Maybe a friend says something simple, but it stays with you. Maybe a sermon feels like it's just for you, answering a question you never said out loud. Or maybe a stranger's kind words lift your spirit, right when you need it most.

A lot of people expect God's voice to be loud, like thunder from heaven. But often, He speaks through people. Sometimes through pastors and prophets, but other times, through ordinary people in everyday moments.

God can use anyone to deliver a message just for you. The key is learning to listen.

What Is Hearing God Through Others?

God uses people to speak His heart. Whether through preaching, one-on-one conversation, or prophetic messages, the Holy Spirit can breathe through another's words to bring clarity, comfort, or direction.

This method isn't about elevating people. It's about recognizing that God can and does speak through yielded vessels.

> *You are blessed, Simon son of John, because my Father in heaven has revealed this to you. You did not learn this from any human being." – Matthew 16:17 (NLT)*

Not everything people say is from God—but God does speak this way.

Why Does God Speak Through Others?

1. To Deliver Timely Encouragement

God often sends someone to speak the very encouragement you've been needing, even if they don't know it.

> *Anxiety in a man's heart weighs it down, but a good word makes it glad." – Proverbs 12:25*

2. To Confirm What You've Been Hearing

Sometimes you're unsure if what you sensed was truly from God until someone unknowingly says the same thing.

> *Every matter must be established by the testimony of two or three witnesses." – 2 Corinthians 13:1*

3. To Deliver Prophetic Guidance

God may choose to deliver a specific message, warning, or insight through someone operating in prophecy.

> *Next year at this time you will be holding a son..."*
> *– 2 Kings 4:16*

4. To Challenge or Correct with Love

God also uses others to gently confront or correct us.

> *Faithful are the wounds of a friend." – Proverbs 27:6*

How God Might Speak to You Through Others

Through Preaching or Teaching – During a sermon, one phrase may strike your spirit and feel like God Himself is speaking.

Acts 2:37 – "When they heard this, they were pierced to the heart."

Pay attention to conviction, clarity, or confirmation.

Through Casual Conversations – A coworker, friend, or stranger might say something that suddenly answers what you've been wrestling with.

Luke 24:32 – "Didn't our hearts burn within us... while he was talking with us?"

God often uses the ordinary to say the extraordinary.

Through Prophecy or Word of Knowledge – God may give someone insight about your situation that they couldn't know naturally.

John 4:18 – "You have had five husbands..."

Prophetic words are not fortune-telling. They're Spirit-led revelations.

Through a Child or the Unexpected – Sometimes it's not who you expect. Stay open.

2 Kings 5:3 – "If only my master would see the prophet..." (spoken by a servant girl)

God can use anyone willing.

BIBLICAL EXAMPLE – Elisha Speaks to the Barren Woman

In 2 Kings 4:16-17, the prophet Elisha told a Shunammite woman, "Next year at this time you will be holding a son in your arms." Her reaction was emotional: "No, my lord! Don't deceive me and get my hopes up like that."

Why? Because she had long given up hope. But sure enough, the next year, she bore a child just as the man of God had said. He used a human vessel to deliver a divine promise and fulfilled it.

REAL LIFE RESULT - How A Sermon Led to My Marriage

I thought I had lost my chance at true love.

The relationship I had invested in for years was gone, and it was my fault. The memories haunted me. I replayed every moment, every mistake, every lost opportunity. Sleepless nights turned into desperate attempts to fix what was broken. I drove long distances, sent gifts and cards, tried everything to restore what was lost. But nothing worked. She had moved on.

Then, one Sunday, my pastor preached a sermon about letting go and beginning again. His words weren't just a general message. They felt like they were spoken directly to me. It was as if God Himself was telling me, **_"It's time to move forward."**_

At first, I resisted. _Move forward to what?_ How could I just walk away after all the years I had invested? But I couldn't ignore what I had heard. The next day, I made the decision. I let go, fully and completely. No more calls, no more lingering thoughts, no more punishing myself. If God was calling me to begin again, I would trust Him.

I didn't know when I would find love again. Or if it would ever compare to what I had before. But then, it happened.

Just three weeks later, I met the woman God had prepared for me. It was as if heaven had been waiting for me to take that step of obedience. She was more than I could have imagined. More attractive, more kindness, more joy, more love than I thought possible. It felt too good to be true, yet it was undeniably real.

Within two months, we were married. And now, over 22 years later, we remain inseparable, deeply in love. More of this story and other inspiring stories about not giving up are in my book "Before I Give Up." You can get a copy via this link. **https://a.co/d/5YNgKgZ

How to Position Yourself to Hear God Through Others

- Prepare your heart before sermons. Ask God to speak.
- Don't dismiss someone because of age, title, status or personal limitations.
- Journal what resonates with your spirit in your own words.
- Have an open mind. Be ready to change.
- ear sermons again to get "your own word" if necessary.

Best Practices for Discernment

- Test every word from individuals with Scripture. (1 Thessalonians 5:21)
- Journal what stands out during sermons or conversations.
- Don't pay for prophecies.
- Let peace be your guide—if it brings fear or pressure, pause.
- Get wise counsel before acting on major words.
- Beware of emotional manipulation or guilt-based messages.

Reflective Bridge

Was that encouragement from your friend... that quote from the sermon... that "random" conversation... really God all along? Maybe you've been hearing God through others you just didn't recognize His voice.

Encouragement

God knows how to get your attention. If He used a donkey to speak to Balaam, He could use anyone to reach you. Stay sensitive, stay humble, and stay listening.

Clarity is possible when you recognize His voice in unexpected places.

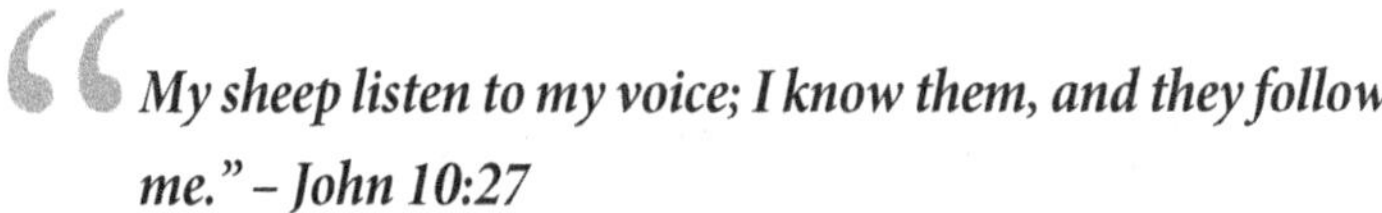

> *My sheep listen to my voice; I know them, and they follow me." – John 10:27*

Reflection Questions

1. Has someone ever said something that felt like God was speaking directly to you?
2. Have you dismissed people God may have used to speak into your life?
3. How can you be more attentive to God's voice through others?

Closing Prayer

"Father, open my ears to Your voice through others. Remove pride, distraction, or doubt that might cause me to miss You. Help me test what I hear with wisdom and Scripture. Use people around me to confirm, guide, and speak truth to my heart. In Jesus' name, Amen."

CHAPTER 17

Hearing the Voice of God Through Songs or Hymns

"When the musician played, the hand of the Lord came upon him."

– 2 KINGS 3:15

You pray, seeking clarity, hoping to hear **God's voice** clearly. But instead of a spoken answer, **a song rises in your spirit**. At first, you dismiss it. Just a tune, maybe a random memory. But what if it's not random? What if the melody is the very message God is sending you?

God is too great to be limited to words alone. He often speaks through melodies, lyrics, and the emotions stirred by a hymn. Some of the deepest moments of divine communication happen unexpectedly. Through songs we haven't heard in years or hymns that suddenly surface in our hearts.

Music is more than sound—it's a spiritual language, a way God speaks, comforts, and guides His people. Let's explore how He uses songs and hymns to reach us—and how you can start listening with your heart.

Maybe that song you keep hearing is God answering in tune.

What Is Hearing God's Voice Through Songs or Hymns?

God can speak through the melody, lyrics, or even the emotions a song evokes. This might happen in a quiet moment of prayer, during a worship service, or unexpectedly while doing everyday tasks.

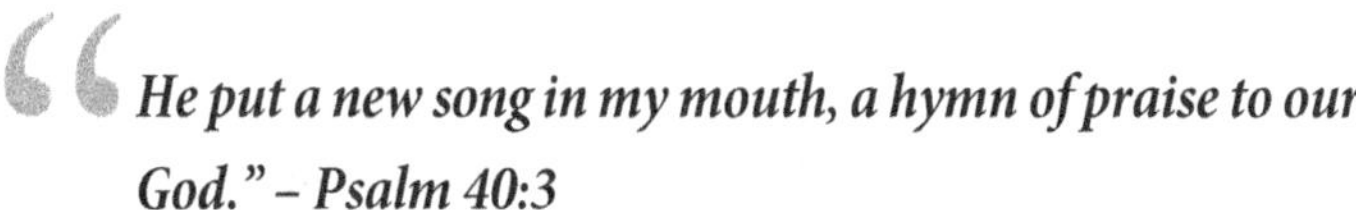

He put a new song in my mouth, a hymn of praise to our God." – Psalm 40:3

This reminds us that songs can be divine messages, placed directly in our spirits.

Why Does God Speak Through Songs and Hymns?

1. To Answer Your Prayers - The lyrics may say what you need to hear.
2. To Bring Comfort and Peace - Songs often carry God's presence, reminding you that He is near.
3. To Guide or Redirect -The emotions stirred may reveal His leading pointing you back to truth or away from confusion.
4. To Unlock Spiritual Sensitivity -Songs stir the spirit and open you to hear more clearly.

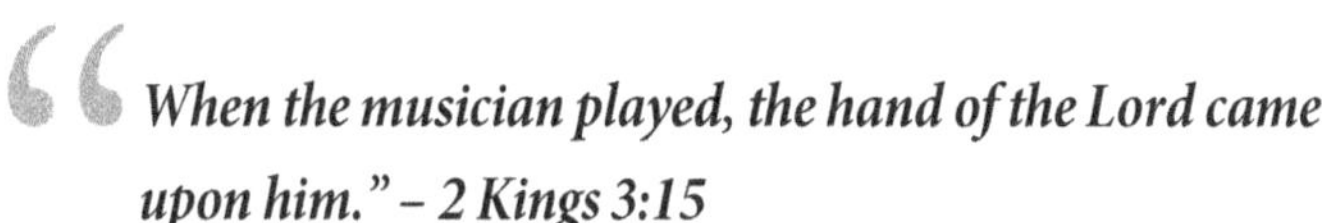

When the musician played, the hand of the Lord came upon him." – 2 Kings 3:15

How God Might Speak to You Through Songs

1. **Through Lyrics** – Have you ever had a song or hymn suddenly surface in your mind? One you haven't thought of in years? As you sing it or reflect on the lyrics, you may realize God is speaking directly to your situation.

For example, if you're feeling discouraged and suddenly remember:

"Great is Thy faithfulness, O God my Father."

It is God reminding you of His unwavering faithfulness to you. He sees you.

2. **Through Emotion** – Sometimes, it's not the lyrics, but the feelings the song evokes. A hymn may bring back memories of **a time when God was especially close. God is reminding you that His presence has never left you.

3. **Through Peace** – A song can carry **a supernatural peace **especially when you've been praying for answers but hearing nothing in return. Suddenly, a song surfaces, calming your anxious heart. That peace is God's way of answering your prayer without words.

4. **As a Pathway** – Music positions you to hear more clearly. Did you know that music can unlock deeper spiritual experiences?

   In 2 Kings 3:15, Elisha requested a musician, and "when the musician played, the hand of the Lord came upon him." Music can position your spirit to receive divine revelation, **whether through prayer, scripture, or even prophecy.

BIBLICAL EXAMPLE – Songs of Deliverance and Revelation

In Acts 16:25-26, Paul and Silas were imprisoned, wounded and bound. Yet, "about midnight, they were praying and singing hymns to God."

Their worship didn't just move heaven. It shook the earth. A violent earthquake broke their chains and flung the prison doors open. God responded not just to their prayers but to their song.

This reveals something powerful: when we sing, we create a divine atmosphere where God can move, speak, and act.

Sometimes, a breakthrough comes not when we ask, but when we sing.

REAL LIFE RESULT – When God Spoke to Me Through a Song

As I entered a new season in my life, I sensed God leading me in a specific direction. First, certain scriptures began standing out to me. Stories of miracles in the book of Acts. Then, a deep stirring grew within me, challenging me to shift my mindset about impossibilities.

And then, God spoke through a song.

One night, I had a dream. In it, I saw a woman I knew well someone who had struggled with barrenness for decades and now has a daughter. In the dream, she was singing a song, and her daughter, the child she once believed impossible, was following behind her.

I woke up singing the very song she had sung:

"Nothing is impossible when you put your trust in God..."

Day after day, the song returned to my memory. Every time I sang it, meditated on the lyrics, and let the words fill my heart, my faith was strengthened. My prayers became bold. My belief in God's power grew. And soon after, I prayed for difficult situations and saw answers.

Hearing God through songs is real. He uses melodies, lyrics, and moments of worship to remind us of His truth. When a song stays in your spirit, don't dismiss it. It may be God's voice, encouraging you, leading you, and filling you with faith.

Sometimes God doesn't say something new. He just sings it again.*

How to Position Yourself to Hear God Through Songs or Hymns

If you want to recognize God's voice through music, here are some ways to tune your heart to Him:

- Pay attention when a song suddenly enters your spirit – It may carry a message.
- Reflect on the lyrics – Ask yourself, *Is God answering me through these words?*
- Sing worship songs often – This positions your heart to receive revelation.
- Notice your emotional response – How do you feel when the song plays?
- Use songs to deepen your prayer – Worship creates an atmosphere where God's voice is clearer.

Be still after a song—God may have more to say.

Best Practices for Discernment

- Test songs with Scripture. Lyrics should align with truth.
- Don't chase emotionalism. Spirit-led worship brings peace, not hype.
- Capture moments. Journal when songs bring clarity.
- Don't ignore repetition. If a song keeps resurfacing, pay attention.
- Let worship soften your heart. It prepares you to receive.

Reflective Bridge

Has a melody been chasing you lately? Has a hymn surfaced from years ago and suddenly made sense? What if the music in your mind is actually a message from God? No more guessing. Hear God clearly—even in song.

Encouragement

If God created sound, rhythm, and voice, why wouldn't He use them to speak?

Don't dismiss the songs that rise up without warning. Don't ignore the chorus that calms your soul.

God is always speaking. Sometimes, He sings. "The Lord your God...will rejoice over you with singing." Zephaniah 3:17. NKJV.

Reflection Questions

1. What's a song that God has used to speak to you in the past?
2. How can you create space to hear Him through worship?
3. Is there a lyric that keeps coming back to you lately?

Closing Prayer

"Lord, open my ears and heart to hear Your voice in music. Let the songs that rise in my spirit carry Your truth. Teach me to listen even when the words are sung. Use melodies and hymns to comfort, guide, and confirm. I trust You to speak. In Jesus' name, Amen."

CHAPTER 18

Hearing God's Voice Through Books

"Your word is a lamp to my feet and a light to my path."

– PSALM 119:105

Many people who struggle with hearing God's voice wonder if He speaks at all. They've done everything they could do but it appears it is dead silence. If that's you, I want you to know something: you are not alone. I have been there. He is still speaking. You just need to know where to look.

One of the ways God communicates is through books. You might be thinking, Books? Really? Yes! God has always used written words to communicate with His people. The Bible itself is proof of that! But beyond the Bible, God can also speak through devotionals, testimonies, Christian teachings, and even stories that reflect His truth. In fact, I believe the Lord is speaking to you through this book.

What if that book on your shelf has been carrying God's voice all along?

What Is Hearing God Through Books?

Hearing God through books means experiencing divine communication as you read. Books can carry wisdom, comfort, correction, or encouragement. Some may echo Scripture, others may stir your spirit with timely truths.

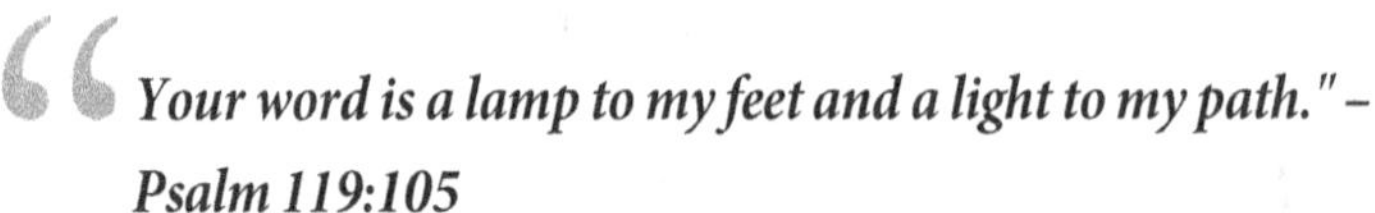

> *Your word is a lamp to my feet and a light to my path." –*
> *Psalm 119:105*

Not every book is God-breathed—but God does breathe through books.

Why Does God Speak Through Books?

1. To Illuminate Scripture

Books that explain the Bible such as devotionals and commentaries can help you understand God's word clearer in a personal and deeper way. They break down complex ideas into simple truths, making it easier to apply them to your life.

2. To Build Your Faith

Reading about someone else's journey can remind you that God is working in your life too. Testimonies show us that God is faithful, and they encourage us to trust Him in our own struggles.

3. To Offer Teaching and Wisdom

Through books, God gives you keys to spiritual growth and direction. Books on faith, prayer, and spiritual growth can give you wisdom for your own walk with God. They provide practical steps to help you grow spiritually and hear God more clearly.

4. To Deliver Truth Through Story

Fiction and narratives can hold hidden treasures of divine insight. Even stories can carry messages of hope, redemption, and God's love. Many Christian novels weave biblical truths into their narratives, helping us see God's heart in a fresh way.

God still speaks today in the same ways He did in Scripture—and He still writes through people.

How God Might Speak to You Through Books

1. **Through a Specific Passage** – One chapter or line may feel like it's speaking directly to you. Pay attention to what jumps out or stirs your spirit.

2. **Through Scripture Illumination** – A Bible-based book may unlock fresh understanding.
   Luke 24:45 – "Then he opened their minds to understand the Scriptures."

3. **Through Emotional Resonance** – Tears, conviction, peace, or excitement while reading may be signals of God speaking.

4. **Through an Unexpected Quote** – A line that confirms a prayer or answers a question.

5. ****Through Other Confirmation** - Sometimes, what you read in a book would be in a seed form. As you open your heart and water it with meditation, and prayers, God may bring confirmation through another means for example, dreams or visions.

BIBLICAL EXAMPLE – Daniel's Revelation from Scrolls

In Daniel 9:2, the prophet Daniel said he "understood by the books" that the desolation of Jerusalem would last seventy years. He discovered this not by a vision or voice, but by reading the writings of Jeremiah the prophet.

God used Jeremiah's scrolls—a written document—to deliver revelation and lead Daniel to intercede for Israel.

This reminds us that sometimes, divine direction is hidden in pages already written.

REAL LIFE RESULT- A Book That Shifted My Heart

Every year, I commit to **30 days of fasting and prayer**, seeking God's direction. But this time, when I reached **day 30**, I hadn't seen the breakthrough I expected—so I kept going.

During my prayers, **God led me to read** *Good Morning, Holy Spirit* by **Pastor Benny Hinn**. At first, I didn't think much of it. But as I read, something **deeply changed** within me.

I had started my fast praying for **God to fulfill His promises** in my life and ministry. But as I continued reading, my desires completely **shifted**. Instead of focusing on results, **I just wanted more of the Holy Spirit**. My goals, my ambitions, even in ministry—faded into the background.

The next day, **God spoke to me audibly in my heart and through a vision**. He said:

"An effective ministry comes through crushing. The oil from your suffering releases a fragrance that makes ministry powerful. Like olive oil under pressure—you are caged in, pressed, and broken. That brokenness is what I use. Strength alone will not make a ministry effective."

The book had **prepared my heart** to receive this truth. I realized that **the delays and challenges** I had been facing weren't obstacles—they were part of **God's refining process**.

Sometimes, God positions a book in our lives not just for knowledge, but to speak to us. To awaken something new within us. That's what *Good Morning, Holy Spirit* did for me. It shifted my focus from achievement to intimacy with God, transforming how I walk with Him today.

How to Position Yourself to Hear God Through Books

- Be intentional—don't just read, ask God to speak before you start.
- Choose wisely—pick books rooted in Scripture and truth.
- Keep a journal—write down any impressions or confirmations.
- Share with others—sometimes God confirms His word through community.
- Reread—sometimes the message becomes clearer the second time.

Best Practices for Discernment

- Test every message with Scripture.
- Don't idolize authors. Only God is infallible.
- Watch for fruit. Does the book produce peace, clarity, repentance?
- Be wary of hype-driven content. Truth doesn't need theatrics.
- Let the Holy Spirit guide your reading list.

Callout: God confirms what He initiates.

Reflective Bridge

Have you heard a passage that gripped your heart, the line that wouldn't let go? Maybe God has already been speaking to you through the books you read. No more guessing. Hear Him clearly.

Encouragement

God is not limited to one method. If He used prophets to write Scripture, He could use writers to echo His heart. Don't dismiss the book that calls to you—it might carry heaven's answer.

God's voice may be printed—but it still lives.

Reflection Questions

1. Have you ever read a book that felt like God was speaking directly to you?
2. What kinds of books stir your faith or bring you peace?
3. Is there a book on your shelf you feel nudged to pick up again?

Closing Prayer

"Lord, thank You for speaking through words written and preserved. Open my heart to hear You as I read. Use books, verses, and stories to draw me closer to Your heart. Let the truths I read become the direction I live. In Jesus' name, Amen."

CHAPTER 19

Hearing God's Voice Through Audible Voice

"This is my beloved Son, in whom I am well pleased."

– MATTHEW 3:17

When most people say they want to hear God's voice, they often mean *audibly*. A voice they can hear as clearly as if someone were standing in the room. But many who desire this have grown frustrated. *"Why can't I hear Him like others do? Am I doing something wrong?"*

If that's you, take a deep breath: **you are not broken, forgotten, or spiritually deaf.** God still speaks in audible ways. Just not always how we expect.

You were never meant to guess. Let's explore how God speaks audibly, and what to look for.

What if the voice you thought was your own—was actually His all along?

What Is the Audible Voice of God?

Hearing the audible voice of God means perceiving His words in a way that mimics or mirrors human hearing. Sometimes it's an external voice; other times, it's a sound you "hear" within—but with the same clarity and weight of spoken words.

Then I heard the voice of the Lord saying, 'Whom shall I send?'" – Isaiah 6:8

Not every sound is sacred, but God still speaks out loud.

Why Does God Speak Audibly?

1. To Give Clear, Unmistakable Direction

Sometimes God chooses an audible voice when He needs to get your full attention.

2. To Interrupt in Critical Moments

Audible moments often come in crises, transitions, or divine assignments.

3. To Establish Relationship

Sometimes God speaks audibly to establish a relationship just like He did with many people in bible.

4. To Confirm Identity or Calling

He speaks aloud to affirm who you are and where He's sending you.

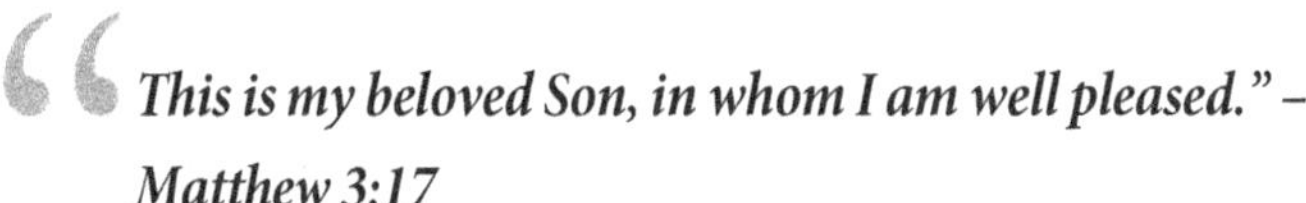

This is my beloved Son, in whom I am well pleased." – Matthew 3:17

God still speaks today in the same ways He did in Scripture.

How God Might Speak to You Audibly

1. **Whisper in the Ear** – A still, quiet voice that feels like someone gently speaking into your ear. It might seem external, but no one else hears it. God might call your name, give a warning, or a short

instruction. In some people they hear it in the ears. Others, it appears the sound is coming just in the little section or hollow behind the outer ear. The voice is definite. It could take a bit to get used to the voice.

2. **Echo Within the Mind** – Sometimes it sounds like a voice inside your head but it's not your own thoughts. The sound is distinct, weighty, and doesn't fade like normal thoughts do.

3. **Room-Filling Voice** – A few have described hearing God like thunder or a voice that seems to fill the air. It may cause trembling or awe, like in John 12:28-29, where some thought they heard thunder but it was God's voice.

4. **Audible But No Input (Mimic Hearing)** – God can bypass the natural ear, sending the sound directly into your consciousness. You didn't hear it with your ears, but your brain registers it like you did. This is what we might call "mimic hearing."

5. **Voice Sound** - nThe sound or tone of the voice of God could assume any distinct tone or sound. However, sometimes, it could take on the tone or sound or voice of a minister of God that you highly respect and honor or even your pastor.

Even if no one else hears it—God still spoke.

BIBLICAL EXAMPLE – Samuel Hears God's Voice (1 Samuel 3)

There are several examples of people hearing the voice of God in the bible. One such example is Samuel. Samuel was sleeping in the temple, where the ark of God was kept. Suddenly, he heard a voice calling his name, *"Samuel!"*He ran to Eli the priest, thinking it was him. This happened three times until Eli realized it was the Lord calling the boy.

"Then the Lord came and stood and called as at other times, 'Samuel! Samuel!' And Samuel said, 'Speak, for Your servant is listening.'" – 1 Samuel 3:10

Samuel had never heard God's voice before, so he thought it was Eli speaking. But God had called him directly, in a way he could recognize. I believe He used Eli's voice. Samuel had to learn how to recognize it. Though a familiar voice, he had to learn to listen to understand His message clearly.

REAL LIFE RESULT – When God Whispered in My Ear

I have heard several moments of hearing God's audible voice.

A few years ago, I went through a very difficult time. God had shown me a glimpse of my future, giving me hope. But as time passed, instead of moving closer to His promises, my life seemed to go in the opposite direction.

I did everything I could think of to fix my situation, but nothing worked. In fact, things got worse. I kept holding on to God's promises, but it felt like everything around me was falling apart.

Then, early one Saturday morning, as I lay in bed struggling with my thoughts, I heard a voice in my ear. Clear and reassuring. It was God.

He said, **"And the affliction which thou suffer in thy days shall not be counted as affliction."**

Those words filled my heart with peace. God saw my pain. He understood what I was going through. He was reminding me that I was never alone. His voice comforted me like a healing touch.

Many believers go through seasons of struggle, wondering if God hears them. Sometimes, when we don't hear His voice, doubt creeps in. But as we have already discussed in previous chapters, God speaks through varied means. An audible voice is just one of them. He is always near.

How to Position Yourself to Hear God Audibly

Read and study the bible regularly. Samuel was sleeping in the temple near the Ark of the covenant where God speaks from. **

Tune out the noise – Quiet your environment and spirit.

Pray with expectation – Ask Him to speak—and wait.

Pay attention in still moments – Many hear Him while resting or just waking.

Write what you hear – Sometimes writing helps you recognize what was truly God.

Avoid pressure – Don't force it. God speaks in His time.

Best Practices for Discernment

- Test what you hear with Scripture.
- Obey the Word – The quicker you obey God, the easier it is to discern His voice.
- Ask for confirmation. He often affirms what He speaks.
- Don't act on fear-based voices. God's voice brings peace.
- Be accountable. Share what you heard with a trusted believer.
- Seek closer relationship with God. It is tempting to seek voice and not God.

Reflective Bridge

Was that voice in the night, so clear, so unexpected really your imagination? **You're not guessing. You're being guided.**

Final Encouragement

You may not hear thunder or a voice echo through your walls, but if God chooses to speak audibly, it will be unmistakable. Stay open. Stay ready.

God's voice can still be heard—with your heart, your spirit, and sometimes, your ears.

Reflection Questions

1. Have you ever heard a voice that seemed to come from outside your thoughts?
2. What emotions did it stir—peace, fear, clarity?
3. Are you willing to let God speak in whatever way He chooses?

Closing Prayer

"Father, I long to hear Your voice—however You choose to speak. If You whisper, let me recognize it. If You thunder, let me not be afraid. Tune my ears and heart to know Your sound. In Jesus' name, Amen."

CHAPTER 20

Hearing God's Voice Through Angels

"Hurry! Take your wife and your two daughters who are here, or you will be swept away..."

– GENESIS 19:15

Have you been helped by an angel and didn't know it?

You're driving on the highway, and suddenly as you are turning a curve, you almost run into a semi-trailer stuck in the middle of the highway. You are within a hair's breadth. Just as you thought all hope was lost, you experienced an unexplainable rescue right when you needed it most. What if that wasn't coincidence? What if it was your angel, sent on assignment from God?

God still sends angels, and they carry out His voice.

What Is Hearing God Through Angels?

God speaks through angels. They are His divine messengers and servants, and so they obey Him. If you are a child of God, you also have an angel assigned to you. When so ordered by God, they're protectors, messengers, healers, and deliverers to you. Sometimes they appear in dreams, sometimes physically, and other times they operate invisibly behind the scenes. Hebrews 1:14 (NLT) reminds us:

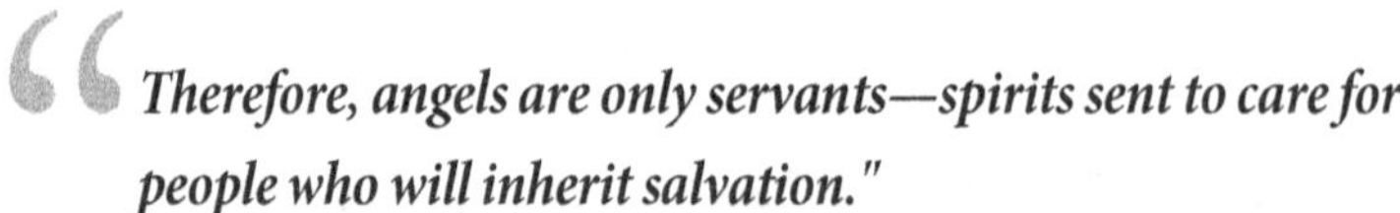

> *Therefore, angels are only servants—spirits sent to care for people who will inherit salvation."*

Majority of the time you may not see your angel. In fact, unless God opens your spiritual eyes, you may not see the angel assigned to you throughout your lifetime. But he is always there with you.

Not every supernatural experience is from God—but God does still send angels.

Why Does God Speak Through Angels?

Beyond your personal angel, the Lord may also on occasions send other angels from His presence on special assignment to you. Most of the time, if you see an angel, he has been dispatched by God. Some of their assignments are below.

1. To Deliver Urgent Instructions

Sometimes God sends His angels with time-sensitive instructions. For example, an angel who told Joseph to flee to Egypt with baby Jesus (Matthew 2:13).

2. To Provide Supernatural Protection

Psalm 91:11 says God gives angels charge over us. Many miraculous escapes or near misses are the unseen work of angels.

3. To Launch or Affirm Ministry Assignments

Also, angels often appear when someone is being sent into divine purpose—such as Gideon, Mary, or Paul.

4. To Reveal Answers To Difficult Questions

At times when God wants to give an answer to questions that defy human understanding an angel may appear. **For example, if you have been** praying to God for a business idea, He could send an angel to teach you the business idea. If you are in medical field, He could send an angel to teach you a cure.

How God Might Speak to You Through Angels

There are two major ways angels may appear to you. **Disguised or Undisguised.**

Disguised - This means the angel appears like a regular human being of any race. This is probably why many people do not recognize angels. (Hebrews 13:2)**

Undisguised - This is when the angel appears in his glorious majesty. Because angels are supernatural beings, their glorious appearance can frighten human beings. That is why one of the first few words an undisguised angel may say to you is fear not.

Below are some of the ways through which God may be communicating through His angels to you.

- **In Dreams** – One of the common places to see an angel is in a dream. Like Joseph, you may receive direction from an angel in your dreams (Matthew 2:13).
- **Through Visions or Trances** – Angels may also appear to you in open visions, night vision or other types of visions or trances with messages, warnings, or encouragement such as with apostle Paul (Acts 27:23).
- **Disguised as People** – Hebrews 13:2 tells us some have "entertained angels unaware." You may interact with a complete stranger who is an angel. Sometimes, God sends angels disguised as regular people in answer to your prayers. They disguise themselves as people needing help. And when the help is given,

they release a life-changing blessing in answer to your prayers. This was how Abraham received Isaac, his promised child (Genesis 18).

- **In Physical Form** – Though rare, God also allow His angels to appear clearly, physically to you often beginning with: *"Do not be afraid."* In the book of Judges 6:12, it tells us that an angel appeared to Gideon. Also, if an angel appears to you in physical form, he may have wings or not. Not all angels have wings.

- **Through Miraculous Intervention** – This is perhaps the most common means of God sending angels to you. Think about many dangers the Lord has rescued you from? These are activities of angels. They maybe hidden from your physical eyes, but actively communicating with you through their actions in your favor.

- **Performing Healing** - God could also use an angel to heal you especially of conditions that seems to have no cure. There are several testimonies of an angel showing up and performing surgery on some people while they sleep.

You don't always have to see the angel to receive the message.

BIBLICAL EXAMPLE – Angelic Intervention for Lot

In Genesis 19, the city of Sodom had reached its limit of wickedness, and God's judgment was imminent. Yet in His mercy, He sent two angels to the house of Lot, a righteous man who lived among the people.

The angels arrived in the evening and were welcomed by Lot. But soon, a mob of wicked men surrounded the house, demanding access to the visitors. Lot stepped outside, trying to protect them. At that moment, the angels intervened. They pulled Lot back inside and struck the men outside with blindness so they couldn't find the door.

Then the angels delivered a direct message from God:

"Hurry! Take your wife and your two daughters who are here, or you will be swept away..." – Genesis 19:15

Even when Lot hesitated, the angels didn't leave him behind. They physically grabbed his hand, along with the hands of his wife and daughters, and led them out of the city. Their instructions were clear, urgent, and filled with divine mercy.

This reminds us: God sends angels to rescue and redirect when our discernment is weak.

REAL LIFE RESULT – When an Angel Saved My Finances

One of my interactions with an angel was recently. In chapter 1, I wrote that the Lord gave me a message that the U.S. stock market would soon tank. And I was told to stay out of the market for now. How did I know it was the Lord? It was through an angel.

The Lord sent an angel to me in a night vision. He appeared disguised as a regular human being. I knew He was an angel because the Holy Spirit through discerning of spirits told me this is an angel.

Then he began to tell me that the euphoria of U.S. market rising won't last forever. He said the market would soon tank. He advised me to stay on the sidelines for now. He also told me that President Trump would soon a deal with a company. He mentioned the name of the company to me. And he told me the fortunes of that company would rise.

What he said has been happening. I must caution you that this is not investment advice. I am just sharing an encounter that I had.

God still sends angels today to communicate with us when necessary. Majority of the time we don't see them. But it's comforting to know that our Father in heaven has that much love for us.

How to Position Yourself to Hear God Through Angels

- Stay open to supernatural encounters—don't force them, but don't rule them out.
- Develop a closer relationship with the Lord.
- Stay rooted in Scripture—it sharpens your discernment.
- Pay attention to your dreams or visions—write down any encounters or instructions.
- Honor the promptings you sense—God may be speaking through His angels.
- Don't worship angels—worship God who sends them.

Best Practices for Discernment

- Test the message—Does it align with Scripture?
- Test for Worship -If an angel asks for worship, he is not from God.
- Test the angel if needed - Ask him to confess that Jesus is Lord (**1 Corinthians 12:3**).
- Test for inner witness—Does your inner witness agree (Romans 8:16)?
- Test for fruit – Does it bring peace and clarity?
- Test for confirmation—Get confirmation from other sources especially for major decisions.

Reflective Bridge

Have you ever had an unexplainable rescue, a stranger's timely word, or a dream that changed everything? That could be an angel on assignment to you that you didn't realize.

Final Encouragement

God isn't limited by our senses. He still uses angels as messengers, guardians, and guides. If you've longed to hear from Him, stay open. Your answer may arrive with wings.

Reflection Questions

1. Have you ever sensed an angelic encounter?
2. How can you grow more sensitive to God's messengers?
3. What would it look like to trust God's supernatural care in your life?

Closing Prayer

"Father, I thank You for the care You've shown me—even when I couldn't see it. Open my eyes to recognize Your messengers. Let me receive every word, instruction, and comfort You send, even through angels. And help me walk boldly in the assurance that I am never alone. In Jesus' name, Amen."

CHAPTER 21

Hearing God's Voice Through Jesus' Appearance to You

"A light from heaven suddenly shone... Saul! Saul! Why are you persecuting me?"

ACTS 9:3–5

What If Jesus Appeared to You?

As we get to the end of this book, I want to mention another way though not common that God may speak to you. That is Jesus Himself appearing to you. Have you ever wondered if Jesus could appear to you?

It might seem unimaginable, but throughout history and even today, He does appear to individuals. These encounters aren't random; they serve a divine purpose, bringing instruction, reassurance, or revelation.

Jesus can appear undisguised, in His familiar form from the Gospels, or disguised, taking on an unexpected appearance. He may speak to you directly or remain silent, allowing His presence alone to convey His message.

If you've ever longed for a direct encounter with Christ, or wondered if such experiences are possible, let's explore how and why Jesus appears, and what it means when He does.

What Is Jesus' Appearance?

An appearance from Jesus is not just an event. It's a divine communication. It could happen through a vision, dream, trance, or even in the physical realm, where your body and spirit interact with Him directly.

His appearance serves many purposes, including:

- Guiding and instructing – Giving direction for your spiritual journey.
- Reassuring and comforting – Reminding you of His presence in difficult times.
- Commissioning and calling – Assigning you to a higher level of ministry.
- Correcting and warning – Helping you realign with His will.

How Jesus Might Appear to You

There are several ways that the Lord could appear to communicate with you. They are below:

1. Undisguised – As He Walked the Earth

Jesus may appear to you as He was when He lived among us: as a Jewish man, clothed in a flowing white robe, reflecting His biblical identity.

2. Disguised – An Unexpected Form

Jesus may also appear in a form you don't expect. He might come:

- As someone of a different race.
- As a stranger or homeless person.
- As an ordinary person you'd overlook.

Why Does Jesus Appear Disguised?

- To test your heart. Will you recognize Him beyond appearances?

- To break misconceptions about His identity.
- To reveal His presence in unexpected places.

Just as He appeared to disciples on the road to Emmaus, but they didn't recognize Him immediately (Luke 24:15-16), He may appear to you in a way that challenges your expectations.

3. Bright Light – A Blinding Encounter

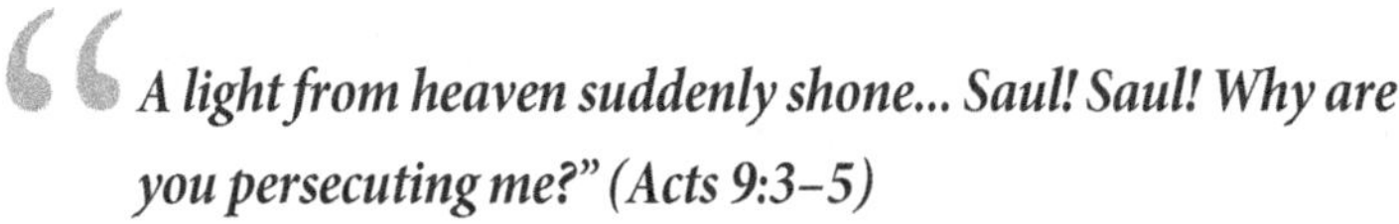

> *A light from heaven suddenly shone... Saul! Saul! Why are you persecuting me?" (Acts 9:3–5)*

One of the most intense ways Jesus can appear is through His radiant glory. It is a light so blinding that you cannot fully see Him but only hear His voice. But it is still a reduced version in intensity of His glorious form. This often happens when God is calling someone to a life-altering ministry such as in Paul's dramatic encounter. **If Jesus appears in a bright, overwhelming light, it usually signals:**

- A life-changing spiritual call.
- A ministry of generational impact.
- Impartation of supernatural gifts with uncommon authority.

Triggers:

1. Salvation of an individual with a unique ministerial call.
2. Commissioning into a higher spiritual assignment.
3. Deep hunger for God, often preceded by fasting and prayer.
4. His divine choosing.

4. Speaking Encounters – A Blinding Encounter

When Jesus appears in this form, He often speaks, giving instructions, warnings, or revelations. He may:

- Guide you in a personal matter – Offering wisdom for life decisions.
- Warn you of a spiritual danger – Correcting mistakes or calling attention to weaknesses.
- Answer your questions – Engaging in direct conversation.
- Give insight into Scripture – Revealing truths that combat deception in the body of Christ.

Example: After His resurrection, Jesus appeared to Paul on the road to Damascus, giving him an entirely new calling (Acts 9:3-5).

Triggers:

1. Intense hunger through prayer.
2. Divine assignment in the Body of Christ.
3. Jesus' own sovereign choice.

5. Non-Speaking Encounter – His Silent Presence

There are times Jesus may appear, but not say a word. Still, His presence communicates everything.

His silent appearance could be:

- To show you that He's with you.
- To express His pleasure in your obedience and faithfulness.
- To prepare you for a coming storm.

Triggers:

1. Long seasons of unanswered prayer.
2. Deep love and sacrifice for Him.
3. His sovereign choice.

Visions, Dreams, Trances, or Real Life

All the above manifestations of Jesus to communicate with you could happen in a dream, vision, trance or in real life. They are all valid. The only difference is the state you are in. When the Lord appears to you in a dream, vision or trance, it is solely your spirit that is communicating with the Lord. Whereas in real life, your body is communicating with Him.

Every appearance is real. Don't discount what happens in the spirit.

REAL LIFE RESULT – When Jesus Appeared to Me

I have had so many encounters with the Lord that I started a Facebook program called *Jesus Is Too Real*. My goal was to call as many people as possible to repentance and help them understand the reality of Jesus. His appearances to me varied. Sometimes bringing encouragement, other times correction. I want to share two of those experiences.

First Visit That I Almost Forgot

It was sometime in January 2012, though I can't remember the exact date. Maybe that was because I was still questioning at the time whether I had really seen Jesus. It seemed too good to be true, even though I had been praying for an encounter.

At the time, my church was holding its annual 30-day fasting and prayer program. My desire for the Lord was strong. So strong that it has continued to this day. I committed to night vigils, praying through the night. Even though I had work the next day, exhaustion never bothered me. My thirst for Jesus outweighed everything else.

Then, one night, as I lay in bed, I was taken into the realm of the Spirit and Jesus appeared to me.

He began speaking. He was not threatening. His appearance was familiar. He looked like the common pictures of Jesus I had seen before. I must admit, I never believed those images were real. I always thought they were just artistic interpretations. But this was how He appeared to me. The way He had walked the earth.

When I woke up, I kept asking myself, *"Was that really Jesus?"* I was so caught up in the experience that I couldn't even remember what He had said. It had been completely unexpected. But the Holy Spirit confirmed that it was the Lord.

We no longer know Him after the flesh..." - 2 Corinthians 5:16)

Jesus Appeared as a Black Man

A few years after His first appearance, the Lord visited me again.

It was an early Saturday morning during our church's annual January fasting and prayer program. The night before, I had spent an hour worshipping the Lord in my living room while my family slept. Those moments alone with God are my favorite. I feel most connected to Him in the stillness of night.

After my usual hour of worship, I was preparing to wrap up when I felt a strong prompting in my spirit. The Lord told me I hadn't worshipped Him enough. So instead of ending my prayer, I entered into a deeper level of praise and worship.

When I worship, time ceases to matter. Day and night feel the same. I don't rush when I'm with the Lord. He is my priority. Sleep becomes secondary. So, I continued worshipping for another hour. Finally, I felt a release in my spirit and went to bed.

Not long after, I was caught up in a vision. In the spirit realm, the Lord appeared to me again. This time, He was disguised as a Black man. It took me a moment to realize who He was. The Holy Spirit whispered to me, *"This is the Lord."*

" *He will glorify Me..." (John 16:14)*

Then Jesus began speaking. I don't think I even let Him finish before I interrupted with questions.

"What is my purpose on earth?"
"Lord, what do You want me to do?"

His response surprised me.

"Many people ask the same question," He said. *"But all I want you to do is be a friend."*

I was taken aback. I had asked Jesus about my life's purpose, expecting something profound—something specific, like a ministry direction or a grand assignment. But He simply wanted me to be a friend.

As I pondered His words, He continued:

"Be a friend to someone. Be My hands and feet. Let people see Me in you."

Then, He showed me something extraordinary. It was as if I was watching a movie—a glimpse into how He had rescued people from trouble. I saw different countries, buildings collapsing, people being saved from disasters, children narrowly escaping dangers that could have taken their lives. But in each scene, Jesus was disguised as an ordinary human being.

How to Position Yourself to Hear God Through Jesus' Appearance

Stay spiritually hungry—create space through fasting and worship.

- Stay rooted in Scripture—He will not appear in contradiction to His Word.
- Be patient—wait for His timing.
- Be humble—don't demand, just desire.
- Journal everything—you may recognize Him more in reflection.

Don't idolize appearances—worship Jesus, not the moment.

Best Practices for Discernment

Not every supernatural appearance is from God. Satan himself disguises as an angel of light (2 Corinthians 11:14). Here's how to test an encounter:

- Discerning of spirits– The gift of discerning of spirits in you will confirm if it is truly Jesus (1 Corinthians 12:10).
- Inner Witness – Does the Holy Spirit's inner witness bear witness in your spirit? (Romans 8:16).
- Ask the person to confess that Jesus is Lord. – False spirits cannot declare Jesus as Lord (1 Corinthians 12:3).
- Ask for 2-3 scriptural confirmations for messages (2 Corinthians 13:1).

Reflective Bridge

Has Jesus already shown up in your life—but you didn't recognize Him?

Maybe He was in the dream you brushed off. Maybe He was that stranger who helped you. Maybe His silent presence carried you through the night. Maybe you've been guessing, but now, you can begin recognizing.

Encouragement

Not everyone will see Jesus physically, and that's okay. He may never appear to you. But His presence in your life is no less real. We are called to walk by faith, not by sight (2 Corinthians 5:7). Whether or not you experience a physical appearance, Jesus is still with you, leading you, and speaking in ways you can hear.

Blessed are those who believe without seeing." – John 20:29

Reflection Questions

1. Have you ever sensed Jesus' presence in a unique way?
2. What would you do differently if He appeared to you?
3. Are you open to how He may choose to reveal Himself?

Closing Prayer

Lord Jesus, I invite You to speak however You choose. Whether through dreams, visions, light, or silence—help me recognize You. I long to hear Your voice and follow You boldly. Even if I never see You with my eyes, help me trust You with my heart. Amen.

CONCLUSION

The Journey Ahead – Doesn't Stop Here

This is the end of the book. But the beginning of a new way of life. You've now learned to:

- Position your heart to listen.
- Discern between His voice and others.
- Watch for His movement in unexpected places.
- Journal and steward your spiritual sensitivity.

You will still have moments of doubt. But now, you have tools. You may still feel unsure—but now you have practice. You might still be surprised. But now, you're aware.

Hearing God was never supposed to feel like a scavenger hunt. It's not reserved for a select few. It's not a reward for being perfect. You were created to commune with God. Hearing Him is your inheritance. And now, you're equipped. Not just with methods—but with faith, discernment, and boldness. You've been taught to recognize His voice, test what you hear, and obey with confidence. The more you listen, the louder He becomes.

Thank you for purchasing this book *"Voice of God – How To Hear It."*

If you enjoyed this book and found some benefit in reading this, I'd like to hear from you. You can reach me below:

Instagram - @Officialjitr

Facebook – Jesusistooreal

Tiktok - @OfficialJesusistooreal

YouTube – JITRONYOUTUBE

Email - ola@jesusistooreal.com

I hope you take some time to post a review on Amazon or any other social platforms. Your feedback and support will help this author greatly improve his writing craft for future projects and make this book even better.

Thank you

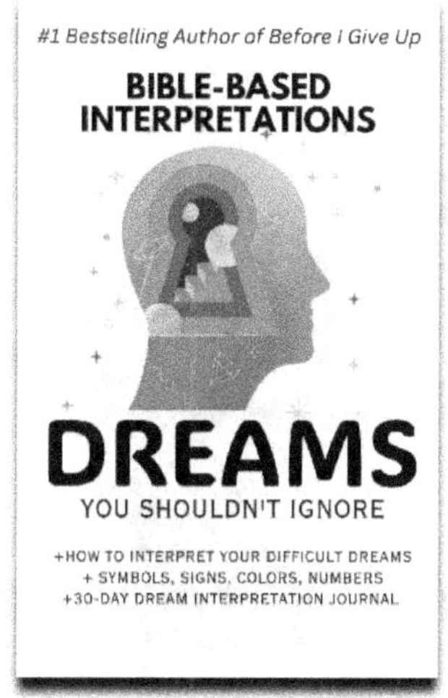

Are your dreams trying to tell you something from God—and you've been ignoring them?

DREAMS YOU SHOULDN'T IGNORE is your clear, Bible-based guide to understanding the divine messages hidden in your sleep. Whether you're seeing symbols, strange numbers, vivid colors, or repeating scenes, this book equips you to decode the language of your dreams through the lens of Scripture.

Inside you'll discover:

- How to interpret your most confusing or disturbing dreams
- The hidden meaning behind symbols, signs, colors, and numbers
- A 30-day guided dream interpretation journal to help you hear God more clearly

If you've ever woken up wondering *"Was that from God?"* — this book is for you. Don't miss another life-changing message by brushing off your dreams. Unlock clarity, purpose, and direction from Heaven. **Stop guessing. Start interpreting. Hear God through your dreams—now.**

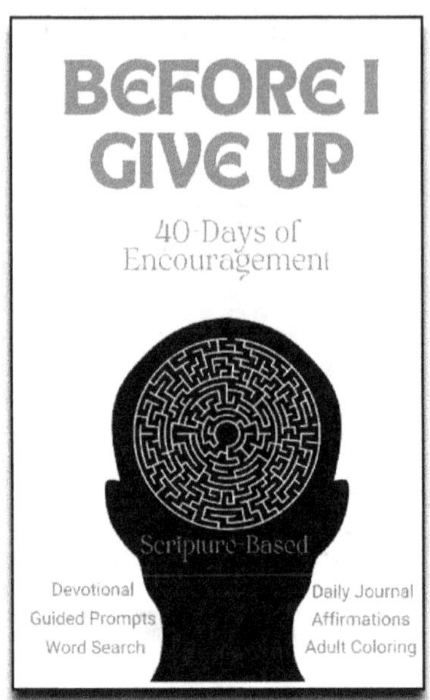

Ola wrote this book for anyone who wants to stop anxiety, overthinking, self-doubt, negativity, and depression for good. Even as a Christian, with a forced smile, he went through dark times and considered ending his life. He experienced intense pain and cried hopelessly every night until he found a solution. From his experience, he shares how to reclaim one's life. This devotional covers 40 various topics like loving yourself, healing trust issues, finding emotional healing, understanding God when life doesn't make sense, creating daily morning routines for success etc.

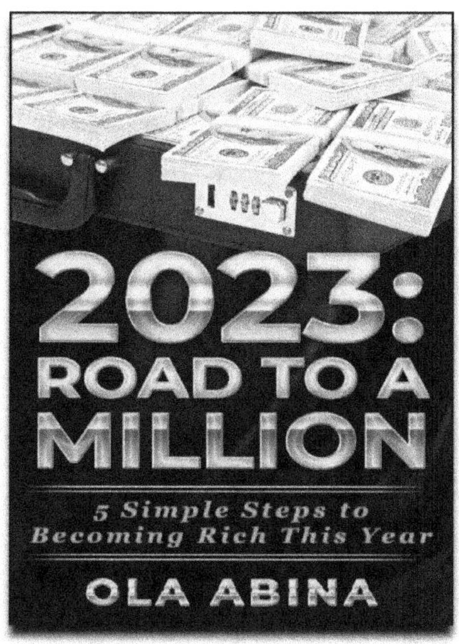

Ola decided to change his financial life after a tragic event forever altered his path for life. With just a few days until his twentieth year at work, he left. He didn't retire. He left. No pension or retirement check safety net. He left his $170,000-per-year job. In this very concise book, Ola created a five-step blueprint that helped him secure financial freedom. The book also reveals the spiritual secret that every person who becomes rich has and how you can tap into it. Starting with basic concepts, you'll learn how to assess your current situation, identify areas of improvement, and start putting plans into action right away. You strive for financial freedom. But how do you get there? This book provides an answer.

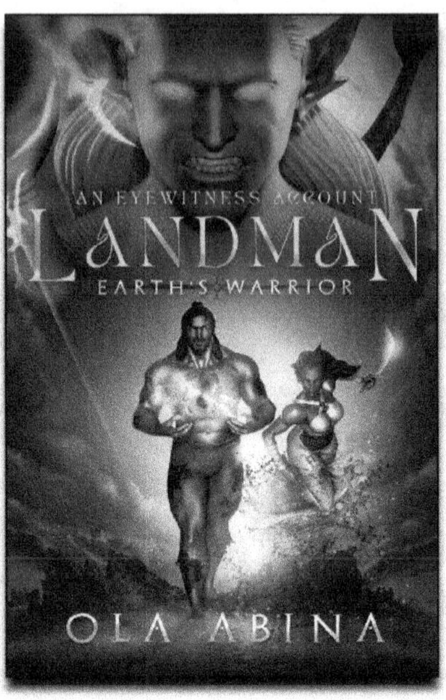

"I have a plan to overthrow the Creator." Gasps spread throughout the audience of angels. Many whispered he would never win, and the Creator would not allow it."

In this thrilling novel, immerse yourself in an intense battle for power and control as Rogue, an ambitious archangel, sets his sights on the Creator's throne. With charm and persuasion, he successfully gathers a formidable army of angels ready to act. However, amidst this divine conflict, there is an unlikely hero, the Landman, who finds himself unwittingly caught in the crossfire. Unbeknownst to him, the Landman holds the key to altering the course of this war. Join him on a journey filled with suspense, thrilling battles, and the ultimate test of courage. Will the Landman rise to the challenge and become the hero mankind desperately needs? Find out in this captivating tale that will keep you on the edge of your seat.

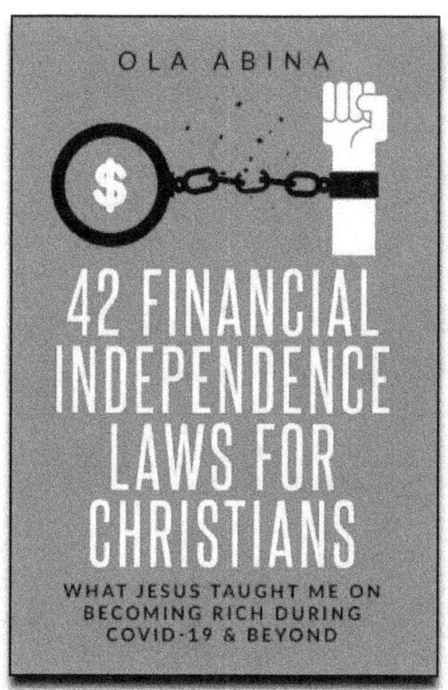

Discover the keys to financial freedom through time-tested biblical principles and cutting-edge strategies! Accelerate your journey to prosperity by learning how to:

- Generate wealth even in times of crisis.
- Apply financial principles that lead to abundance.
- Break free from the shackles of debt.
- Stay ahead of the game by identifying future trends in products and services! Unlock the secrets to a prosperous future and secure your financial well-being today!

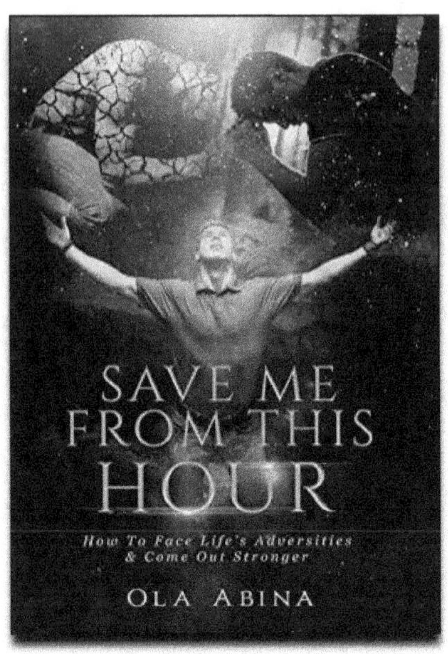

Discover a book that brings hope, empowerment, and healing. Whether you're a victim of your own choices, the actions of others, or simply the unpredictable journey of life itself, this powerful resource offers hope and solace. With engaging stories and powerful insights, this resource is a must-have for anyone who has faced adversity, is currently navigating challenging times, or will inevitably encounter obstacles in the future. Get ready to embrace a dynamic blueprint for facing life's toughest trials, emerging victoriously and stronger than ever before, where every obstacle becomes an opportunity for growth.

ABOUT THE AUTHOR

Olaoluwa "Ola" Abina, most widely known for his international best seller, *Dreams You Shouldn't Ignore,* is an author, publisher, and a well sought after conference speaker. Ola's writing journey began after the sudden demise of his beloved mother, which debuted his first book *Save Me From This Hour – Overcoming Life's Adversities.* In response to overwhelming demand from him for life advice, and dealing with the same issues himself, Ola found a passion for writing on topics about overcoming life's challenges, love, financial freedom and relationships using time-tested biblical solutions. After leaving his full-time job in 2021 to pursue his purpose of becoming a full-time author, Ola released the following books *Landman Earth's Warrior (A work of fiction) and 2023:ROAD TO A MILLION.* His last book, *Dreams You Shouldn't Ignore,* quickly rocketed to success and sold out within a few weeks. Ola's uniqueness lies in using the name and principles of Jesus Christ to solve contemporary problems. As he travels around the world, using these principles, he has seen the lives of hundreds of thousands transformed as he inspires men and women, becoming a voice of hope to those who have lost faith. Ola is the host of "Jesus Is Too Real," a program that uses the name and principles to solve contemporary problems. He currently resides with his family in Baltimore, Maryland.

You can connect with Ola on these platforms:

Instagram - @Officialjitr
Facebook – Jesusistooreal
Tiktok - @OfficialJesusistooreal
YouTube – JITRONYOUTUBE
Email - ola@jesusistooreal.com